Wiltshire
Village Reading Rooms

Ivor Slocombe

HOBNOB PRESS

for the

WILTSHIRE BUILDINGS RECORD

First published in the United Kingdom in 2012
on behalf of the Wiltshire Buildings Record
by The Hobnob Press, PO Box 1838, East Knoyle, Salisbury SP3 6FA.
www.hobnobpress.co.uk

British Library Cataloguing in Publication Data
A catalogue record for this book is available from the British Library.

ISBN 978-0-946418-91-6

Typeset in 11/15 pt Scala. Typesetting and origination by John Chandler
Printed in Great Britain by CPI Antony Rowe

The Wiltshire Buildings Record is a voluntary society and educational charity, with
members in historic Wiltshire and beyond. The archive of the Record, gathered together
since 1979 from fieldwork and from a variety of sources, covers over 15,000 sites
representing buildings of all dates and types. The collection is housed at the Wiltshire &
Swindon History Centre, Cocklebury Road, Chippenham, Wiltshire SN15 3QN, telephone
01249 705508. It is open to the public on Tuesdays, 9 a.m. to 5 p.m.

Also available from Wiltshire Buildings Record:

Wiltshire Farmhouses and Cottages 1500-1850	£6
Wiltshire Farm Buildings 1500-1900	£5
Medieval Houses of Wiltshire	£6
Wiltshire Town Houses 1500-1900	£6
Architects and Building Craftsmen with Work in Wiltshire (Part 1)	£6
Architects and Craftsmen with Work in Wiltshire (Part 2)	£8

All plus £1.50 per copy post and packing.

The Dovecotes and Pigeon Lofts of Wiltshire (J & P McCann)	£14

plus £2.50 per copy post and packing

You can help the Record by allowing us to copy photographs, drawings and any other
information, structural or historical you may have about Wiltshire buildings. Please join
the Record and help to record buildings in your locality or assist us by drawing our
attention to threatened buildings which may be worth recording.

Contents

Colour Plates 1-58 will be found between pages 64 and 65

Preface

A reading room was an important institution in the majority of villages in the late 19th century. Yet, surprisingly, the whole reading room movement and the establishments it produced have been almost entirely neglected by historians. This study of Wiltshire will, it is hoped, fill a gap and demonstrate not only how widespread were the reading rooms but also their importance in both rural education and the impact of the temperance movement.

I am most grateful to a large number of people for their help and encouragement in this project. In particular Dorothy Robertson shared with me some of her earlier research while the staff of the Wiltshire & Swindon History Centre were, as usual, very helpful and pointed me towards unexpected areas of further information. I must also thank my wife for accompanying me on expeditions around the county in search of elusive buildings and for taking most of the photographs in this book.

Many owners of houses which were originally reading rooms have most generously shared their knowledge of the buildings with me and allowed photographs to be taken.

I would like to make special mention of Carole King who has done so much pioneering work on the study of reading rooms in Norfolk and who kindly let me have a copy of her unpublished thesis. I share with her a lasting enthusiasm for this much neglected subject.

IVOR SLOCOMBE

Map of Wiltshire Reading Rooms mentioned in the text.
(Salisbury and Mere are approximately 20 miles or 32 km apart)

The Reading Room Movement

The village reading room movement started in the mid 19th century with new rooms being established until soon after the First World War. There had been literary and scientific institutions from the late 18th century but these were urban, middle class cultural societies. The Mechanics Institutions were also intended for the new industrial artisans with education as their foremost object. Mutual Improvement Societies of working men began to be established in the early 19th century with self-education, mutual support and political discussion which was likely to be liberal if not radical. Although the village reading rooms followed on from these to fill the rural gap, it was a quite distinct movement with a somewhat different rationale. The starting point was to provide an alternative to the public house for the agricultural labourers during the long winter evenings and, as such, was closely linked with the temperance movement. Education also featured largely in the aims of the founders but was never the sole object and recreational games always formed an essential attraction in the reading rooms.

The main impetus for the movement, if not its starting point, is usually taken to be Samuel Best's lecture on 'Village Libraries and Reading Rooms' given in August 1854.[1] He talked somewhat disparagingly about the agricultural labourer saying that 'the intellect of the shepherd of Salisbury Plain, notwithstanding the almost classical position literature has assigned

The Hon and Rev Samuel Best, by Alfred Stevens, c. 1840 (Tate Gallery)

to him, is inferior in intelligence to the sharp witted Yorkshireman whose intellects have been exercised from his earliest boyhood in the great craft of life.' He was probably right in pointing out that young boys going into agriculture had always left school early and the very nature of their occupation did not require much intellectual input. But he also pointed out that agriculture was going through a period of technical and mechanical improvement and it was these very same workers who would be responsible for carrying the developments through. Libraries were essential for taking their education further. The problem was, however, that the workers' cottages were dark and overcrowded and quite unsuitable for taking books home to read. This is why the establishment of a reading room in each village was important. It would also provide the facilities which many were led to seek in the public house.

> There they cannot enjoy the resources without drinking 'for the good of the house'. For this class, the well warmed and well lighted reading room with books and papers will prove the resource they otherwise seek elsewhere. As a further inducement and convenience, where the desire is felt for them, tea and coffee may be readily made to take the place of the beer of the publican ... and for recreation and amusement, the chessboard and the draughtboard may be called in aid and be in harmony with the other pursuits of the workers.'

He concluded:

> We want the library and reading room as a means to an end and that end is the enfranchisement of the intellect of the labouring classes. ..... If we can introduce an intellectual atmosphere into our village, if we can find some counterpoise for the public house and beer shop and lastly, if we can bring together the different classes of which even village life is composed and cement the union by the bond of the intelligence.

It is clear from the lecture that Best was not inventing the idea of the village reading room but was building on the experience of some already in existence. He was a clergyman working and preaching in the Hampshire area and gives examples of reading rooms which had recently been established in some Hampshire and Wiltshire villages. He quotes a village (not named) with a population of about 800, entirely agricultural and situated on the verge of Salisbury Plain. A reading room was established there a year before with £100 raised by a zealous and benevolent promoter. It started with a library of 230 volumes and had 32 subscribers paying 10s. or 6s. annually, 31 at 6d. monthly and 16 at 2d. monthly. Through the kindness of the squire and the activity of the officers, the daily and county papers were taken in. The reading rooms in this area had been promoted by the Hants and Wilts Educational Society[2] whose objects were 'To provide the establishment of libraries and reading rooms and to encourage the spirit of inquiry and improvement by the delivery of lectures on literary and scientific subjects or by the formation of classes.' It maintained an approved list of lecturers, had a stock of diagrams and apparatus for their use, and had the power to make grants in aid of expenses incident on the establishment of reading rooms or the formation of classes.

An early institution similar to the later village reading rooms but in an urban setting was established in Montague Street, Bristol in 1850.[3] It was open five nights a week in premises occupied by the Working Men's Improvement Society and was to be called the People's Reading and Instruction Society. Subscriptions were a penny a week or a shilling a quarter but members of the Mutual Improvement Society were admitted at the reduced rate of 9d a quarter. It was promised copies of the Express London evening paper, the Bristol Mercury, Bristol Times, Inquirer and American Liberator. Another early working man's establishment was founded at Westminster in 1854 by Rev. Malone and Mrs. Buckland, wife of the Dean of Westminster.[4] This was a moderately priced refreshment room (small plate of beef for 3d, tea at 4d a pint) attached to which was a reading room with a library and supply of games which could be used freely by customers. Other people could use the facilities for ½d a time or 2d a week.

Another early advocate of village reading rooms was Lord Stanley. In 1855 he proposed what The Times[5] described as 'an eminently practical and useful scheme, though not altogether new, for facilitating rational recreation and self-culture among the humbler classes in the rural districts of the country, by means of public libraries established at central or salient points of the county, and radiating from them a series of small local reading rooms for every village.' He then went on to illustrate this with a possible scheme for Norfolk. This was considered to be rather controversial and sparked off a lively series of letters. C. St. Denys Moxon, the curate of Fakenham, wrote to oppose the idea of central libraries which, he said, are 'above the masses and useful only to a few'.[6] He wanted, instead, the large landowners to provide good libraries in their own parishes. A more sanguine response came from 'A Country Vicar' [7]who said his parish was 25 miles from London and had a population of 1,700. He had tried to establish a reading room in a warmed and lighted building open every evening. It took a number of daily and local papers together with a library. The subscription was 6d a month to the reading room and library and 3d to the library only but just 20 people had become members.

> Mr. Plums takes his paper at home; Mr. Suet prefers the free and easy with Bell's Life in the parlour at the Crown or Chequers. 'John Hodge' likes the roaring song or the endless yarn in the taproom when he has money, and bores his wife at home when he has none. Those young rascals 'Bill' and 'Tom' will persist in lurking at the street corner to trip up Susan going home with the doctor's beer or in making a party to kick in Mother Jones's door for telling the parson who stole his apples.

He thought the Stanley scheme was too urbanised for the villages. 'Libraries and reading rooms on the town system will be about as much good to the rustic class as roast beef and plum pudding would be to a suckling infant.' He suggests a much more modest plan at least to start with. 'In every country village containing a population of 400, let two decent adjoining rooms be secured with a small kitchen attached. In room 1 every evening from 6 to 9 during the winter season, let there be a good fire and sufficient light. On the table throw a newspaper or two. In the kitchen let there be a decent woman prepared to sell at reasonable prices good tea, coffee, plain biscuits, tobacco and pipes.' If the scheme takes off, then is the time to open the second room with papers, pens and a small supply of books. Another correspondent 'Abnormis Sapiens'[8] also wanted a simpler scheme. He advised three conditions for success:

> The rules must be few and simple; the fewer the better. Our poor people can neither understand nor keep many and complex rules.
> The subscription must be very trifling.
> The books chosen for the library must be cheerful, as well as moral and religious – not merely taken out of the somewhat dry lot published by the worthy S.P.C.K. Society.
> Finally he suggested that all these benevolent undertakings might have greater success if 'we abstain from conspicuously bringing before their notice our kind intentions of moulding and bettering them'.

Opposition to the new reading rooms inevitably came from the landlords of the public houses. Punch[9] published an amusing article in 1861 written in dialect supposedly from 'Phil Potts'. He describes a 'Working Men's Club' set up in his neighbourhood.

> 'Tis to be a Clubb and Reedin Room, comojus and wentilated and all that with the ixpress Vu of makin hof it as comfortable as the Public Ouses. .... They've got a comitty of wurkin Menn a dozen of 'em wot manidges the Afairs of the Clubb. The scripshun is only apeny a Weak.

He encourages Punch to tell the working man to

> dispize imitatin the Swels, with their garricks and Reforms and conservativs and Ragg and Fammishes and its yure opinyun there's nuthin for the wurkin Menn like the good old public ouse where 'e can heat is tripe and Smoak is pipe and tiple is noggin of beer, gin or wot not, and rede the papers into the Bargin, until e reads 'em dubble, and so go ome cumfable to the buzzum of is Fammaly.

Despite these caveats and opposition, there is no doubt that many reading rooms were established across the country in the 1850s. A further boost came in 1862 with the pamphlet published by 'A Country Curate' *A Plea for Reading Rooms in Rural Parishes*. He covers much of the old ground – picturing the crowded cottage with scarcely enough room to contain its numerous inmates. So 'after having a meal, he rushes forth and standing at the corner of a street, becomes a prey to every idle thought and every temptation that assault the unoccupied mind; and, perhaps too, which is the saddest of all, from having no place where to spend the long winter evening, he falls into those habits of intoxication which are the ruin at once of his temporal and spiritual prospects.' Interestingly he introduces a new argument for the church to become involved in the establishment of the new reading rooms. He says that there the local clergyman will have the opportunity to make contact with many who do not go to church and otherwise he would not see. In the end these might be brought to attend a place of worship and, amongst his own congregation, he has noticed that the most regular and attentive are the members of the reading room. He finishes: 'May every village have its reading room as well as its school and its church. They may all be made to work to one end viz. to provide the glory of God by the salvation of man.'

All the evidence suggests that by the 1860s the concept of the village reading room had been widely accepted and endorsed by the local gentry, by the church and not least by leading politicians. This is, perhaps, epitomised in the long speech by William Gladstone, then Chancellor of the Exchequer, at the opening in 1864 of the Working Men's Reading Room at Buckley near Mold.[10] He said that it was no longer necessary to have to argue the merits of such institutions. 'Happily, their utility is generally recognised. They have taken hold upon the mind of the people; they have struck a deep root in many districts of the country; they are spreading and multiplying; they are thriving where they exist in a degree heretofore unknown; they are coming into existence where they don't exist; and their general warrant and justification are complete.'

In the middle of the 19th century there was a parallel campaign, in which Florence Nightingale played a leading part, to provide or improve reading room facilities for soldiers. A letter in the Times[11] in 1856 from C. A. Assheton Craven, Military Chaplain, Second Brigade, First Division, Army in the East, Crimea, explained that he had established a reading room mainly to provide amusement for the soldiers during the winter months and to wean them from the allurements of the canteen. This followed reports of widespread drunkenness amongst the soldiers in the Crimea. He had obtained a hut and provided it with a stove, reading and writing desks and a library of books to make it exceedingly comfortable. He was now appealing for a supply of newspapers and games such as chess and draughts. Florence Nightingale took up the issue after she had returned from the Crimea in about 1860.[12] She then wrote to her old friend, Sidney Herbert, Secretary for War, to ask him to establish a committee of inquiry into what reading room facilities existed in the soldiers' barracks. She was concerned about the 'moral health' of the soldiers and complained that the Chaplains did nothing except making men confess old sins after they had done them. She had evidence that the 'Social Evil' was one third worse than it used to be and worse at Woolwich than at Aldershot. Many in the army simply said that 'men are animals ... all you can do is place the vice under regulation as you do the food'. Florence Nightingale argued that libraries, day rooms and reading rooms with plenty of light and fire, smoking, tea and coffee might not completely stop the evil but it had diminished it where it had been fairly tried. She eventually persuaded Herbert to establish such a committee of inquiry and she then proceeded to write it a very detailed memorandum on what they should look for and what questions they should ask.

Her brief reveals exactly what she thought a reading room should look like and contain. Heat and light were basic essentials for these were absent from the barrack rooms. This is reminiscent of the argument for the village reading rooms and the comparison with the inadequacies of the labourers' cottages. The committee should get information on the amount of fuel issued and the amount required for effective warming. They should ascertain the manner of lighting whether by gas, candles or oil lamps together with the number of candles, gas jets or oil lamps allowed per room. They should also look at the kind of furniture provided for each room and the supply, if any, of maps, plans, charts and prints for the walls. The number of volumes in each library had to be counted, the number and names of newspapers and periodicals and the general character of them and the games and amusements provided. The finances should be looked at including the monthly income arising from subscriptions, penalties, profits on the sale of tea and coffee and how the funds are disposed of. The committee should inquire into the nature of the management of the rooms and try to establish the reasons for the success or want of success. The pay of the librarians should be looked at and whether they possess or wear uniform. Finally there was her somewhat imperious order 'You will make such recommendations on all the points in these instructions as may, in the opinion of the committee, tend to this result.'

It is not clear how successful this campaign was but a letter to the Times in August 1883 from William Tallack[13] suggests that there was still a lot to do. He highlighted the lack of facilities for soldiers so that they came to rely on the canteen which in turn led to drunkenness and associated offences. He wanted the authorities to guard their soldiers against strong temptations which were likely to lead to such painful consequences. One of the best means to attain this end would be a more systematic provision for libraries and reading rooms throughout the army. He also suggested that the Chaplain General and his clergy might join with the local clergy in garrison towns and render help in this direction.

Wiltshire: Foundations

The reading room movement in Wiltshire very much reflected the national movement with the two main aims of an alternative to the public house and a place for the development of education, although there was a difference in emphasis in various places. The incentive at Market Lavington was very strongly about temperance and the official opening in 1865 was celebrated by a tea and then an open discussion in which virtually all the speakers from a wide area talked about the evils of intoxicating drink. At Highworth the chairman, Rev. Norman, also highlighted the importance of the reading room as an alternative to the public house: 'Places where the working men of our villages may meet together for an evening's chat, without being also tempted into an evening's dissipation, ruinous alike in its effects upon body as well as soul.' The particular need for such places because of the inadequacies of the labourers' cottages was referred to in the move to establish the reading room at Salisbury St. Martin's: 'The labouring man, who has but one room for all domestic operations, wants some place of an evening to go to where he can have company and a little relaxation from his heavy work.'

In contrast, Lord Fitzmaurice concentrated on the educational value of reading rooms when opening the five new institutions on the Bowood estate. He emphasised the importance of all men becoming aware of what was happening in the world and having access to a range of views on the great current questions. Interestingly he recommended the Bremhill reading room to take the journal printed by the Agricultural Society. This links closely with the argument made by Best that agricultural labourers would be the ones to implement the great changes in farming and therefore should be better informed about them. Lord Fitzmaurice, although hardly a democrat, was liberal and broad-minded emphasising that the reading room was for all classes and the farmers as well as the labourers. He was backed up at Bremhill by William Carpenter of Calne who had for long campaigned for a reading room in the village. 'He could not see why some of the lads and young men present, if they rightly improved their minds and time, should not rise to some of the most honourable positions in life. He discarded altogether the erroneous ideas of educating a boy according to the station in life he would have to fill as it was impossible for anyone to tell what he might become if he had the means of rising.' He was eminently practical in returning to the farming theme when he commented that a ploughboy and his carter ought to know how many miles they would have to walk in a day if a field was a given length in order to plough three quarters of an acre per day.

In providing newspapers and books, the assumption was that most village labourers could read. This was not so at Ramsbury. Mr. Batson of Parliament Piece recalled that when he came to Ramsbury in 1858 he found the village in a lamentable state of ignorance and a general low sense of morals. He started a reading room with books and newspapers for the tradesmen and lower classes and, although attendance was good, he found few could actually read fluently enough to make use of the material provided. He therefore converted it into a night school. This must have been an exception, for Wiltshire was very well provided in the mid 19th century and virtually every village had some kind of school. The 1858 survey recorded nearly 30,000 children attending some form of day school and another 9,000 going to night school. The total population of the county was then about 270,000 and clearly the majority of children were getting an elementary education. This suggests that a large proportion of the village labourers were likely to be able to read sufficiently to be capable of using the new reading rooms.

The great challenge to the founders of the reading rooms was to strike an appropriate balance between providing a place sufficiently attractive to the labouring classes but at the same time to ensure it was also a place for educational and moral advancement. Recreational facilities had to be provided but these were not to dominate or to be frivolous. At Dilton Marsh, the stated object was to afford members a means of moral and mental improvement, social intercourse and rational recreation. The chairman at Norton Bavant was keen to emphasise that 'this is not a room for idle resort but for instruction, amusement and to pass a leisure hour.' The whole issue was neatly summed up by the chairman at the re-opening of the Wroughton reading room.

The object of the institution was, in the first place, making it a reading room; and, in the second place, making it a recreation room, and the question was how could they make it one or both – or rather both – and make it really serve the purposes they had in view. They wanted to make the young people about the village and neighbourhood feel that there was a place where they could have useful and friendly intercourse with one another and at the same time get instruction from the reading of the newspapers and good books which such an Institution should afford, and also have, at the same time, the advantage of such little recreation as afforded them now in places which were not quite so useful to them, and perhaps a little more detrimental to their welfare.

The one issue on which all agreed, no matter who founded the reading room, it should be non-sectarian and free of all party political discussion and activity.

The dates of the foundation of the Wiltshire reading rooms also echo what seems to have been the national pattern. The first reading rooms were established in the 1850s with the latest ones tailing off after the First World War. The great bulk of the county's reading rooms were built in the 1870s, 1880s and 1890s with the 1890s being the real heyday of their existence. The 'golden year' was 1884 when ten new reading rooms were opened at Ashton Keynes, Broad Hinton, Bromham, Burbage, Calstone Wellington, Foxham, Mere, Shaw and Whitley, West Ashton and Wylye. There is firm evidence of the opening dates for 105 reading rooms, about 60% of the total which existed at one time or another. Many of these were replaced by better buildings at a later date.

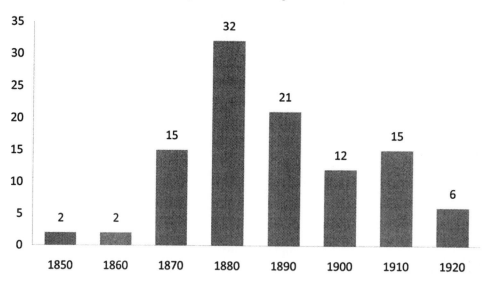

The earliest reading room in the county was probably at Lacock established in 1854. This was on the initiative of Rev. Arthur Bloomfield, vicar of Lacock, supported by a number of the local gentry including William Fox-Talbot of Lacock

Abbey and Captain Gladstone, brother of prime minister William Gladstone. The first reading room at Wroughton was opened in 1859 as part of the Mutual Improvement Society. There was then a gap until 1865 when the very substantial Workmen's Hall was built at Market Lavington mainly with funds left by Edward Saunders. The reading room at Bratton, said in 1867 to have been recently established, was on a much smaller scale, almost certainly in rented rooms, and was perhaps more typical of the majority of small village reading rooms.

At the other end, Collingbourne Kingston, erected in 1938 to commemorate the reign of George V, was the last purpose-built reading room (although there had been an earlier one destroyed by fire in 1936). The object of the Trust was 'for the purpose of physical and mental recreation and social, moral and intellectual development through the medium of reading and recreation rooms, library, lectures, classes, recreations and entertainments or otherwise as may be found expedient.' Although this clearly refers to 'reading room', it was probably little more than the village hall and the building was referred to as such from an early date. The reading room at Turleigh was also something of a 'one-off'. The gift in 1920 by Major Scarth in memory of his wife was called 'The Club' and also housed his personal library.

There was a slight flurry of activity immediately after the end of the First World War. Little Cheverell was established in 1919 in a wooden hut almost certainly one of the many which were sold off by the army from their temporary camps on Salisbury Plain. The Staverton initiative in 1919 also seems to be connected with post-war celebrations and their hut came from the Red Cross hospital in Trowbridge. The Cherhill room was erected as a First World War memorial with ex-YMCA huts from Yatesbury airfield. The wooden hut erected at Marden in 1923 has all the characteristics of the ex-army huts.

One might expect that there would be some connection between the size of the parish and having a reading room. In 1890 Wiltshire had 327 rural parishes, 150 of which were very small with a population of under 300. At some time or another there were at least 170 reading rooms in the county i.e. over half the parishes had one. This is slightly misleading as some places, such as Chitterne with one reading room, were technically two parishes although for all practical purposes it was one community. At the other extreme the parish of Bradford Without included several quite separate communities some of which had their own reading room. It is not surprising to find that most of the larger parishes had a reading room but there is no evidence of one at Colerne or Whiteparish each with a population of over 1000 in 1891. Perhaps more interesting is the fact that

Chilmark

Grittleton

Upavon

Corsley

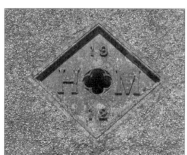

Fonthill Bishop

Derry Hill

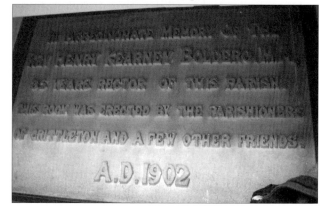

Grittleton (foundation stone)

Wiltshire Datestones and Foundation Stones

Market Lavington

*East Kennett
(foundation stone)*

Holt

Purton

Whitley (foundation stone)

Redlynch (foundation stone)

Foxham

Wiltshire Datestones and Foundation Stones

some of the very smallest parishes could boast a reading room, such as Alvediston, Brixton Deverill, Little Cheverell, Marden, Nomansland and Norton Bavant, each with a population in 1891 of under 200. Perhaps the smallest community was the hamlet of Clevancy in the parish of Hilmarton which consisted simply of two farms. If there is no correlation between size of parish and reading rooms there is also no geographical connection. The reading rooms are spread quite evenly across the county and there is no apparent link with the type of village, its type of agriculture, its industry or social structure. The only common factor is undoubtedly the human one; most reading rooms in Wiltshire were established through the actions of a single benefactor or by a group of local people especially with the leadership or the encouragement of the vicar.

There is no evidence in Wiltshire of groups of working men coming together of their own volition to establish a reading room. It may be, however, that some of the smaller reading rooms in rented cottages could have been formed by working men but this type of foundation was most unlikely to be reported in the press or recorded elsewhere. There is firm evidence about the founders of 78 reading rooms in the county. These may be broadly categorised into:

Aristocracy/gentry/wealthy landowners	55
Local committee/vicar	15
Memorials	4
Charities	4

Undoubtedly it was local, wealthy benefactors who were mostly responsible for building the reading rooms. Some were aristocratic estate owners, in particular Lord Fitzmaurice with his brother, the Marquess of Lansdowne, who provided five reading rooms on their Bowood estate at Bremhill, Calstone Wellington, Charlcutt, Derry Hill and Foxham. The Earl of St. Germans (Latton), Lord Heytesbury (Heytesbury), Lord and Lady Long (Steeple Ashton and West Ashton), the Morrisons of Fonthill (Chilmark and Fonthill Bishop) and Lady Burdett (Ramsbury) were also local benefactors. An early activist was Walter Powell, the son of a wealthy coal-mine owner in South Wales, who had come to live at Dauntsey House near Malmesbury. He became M.P. for Malmesbury and was known as a philanthropist who was responsible for many 'acts of benevolence'. He founded reading rooms at Malmesbury, Great Somerford and Little Somerford. The Fullers of Neston Park were responsible for the reading rooms at the nearby villages of Atworth and Shaw. The small reading room at

Lydiard Millicent and the very large workmen's institute at Purton both came from funds provided by J. H. Sadler of Lydiard House, the latter in memory of his wife's sister. A typical example of this type of benefactor was Mr. Blake of Codford; he simply said that he had long wished to see a reading room established in the village but, as no one came forward, he had decided to build one himself.

In other places it was the vicar who took the lead to form a local committee, often with the support of the larger landowners, to raise funds and acquire a suitable building. This was certainly the case at Dilton Marsh, Fovant, Lacock, Laverstock, Mere, Stratford-sub-Castle, Tisbury, Warminster Sambourne and Wylye. In these and in many other places the vicar took a continuing interest in the local reading room and more often than not became the chairman of the management committee. This emphasises the involvement of the church in the whole reading room movement. There was also a church connection, albeit indirect, in the foundation of the reading room at Broad Chalke in 1911. There the initiative was taken by King's College, Cambridge the patron of the living. In 1909 the treasurer of the college's Social Work Committee wrote to the vicar offering to help pay for a reading room. The committee aimed at sponsoring 'physical and mental training and recreation and social, moral and intellectual development through the medium of reading and recreation rooms, library, lectures, classes and recreation and entertainment or otherwise.' The two-roomed building on a site given by Lord Pembroke was said to be made of bricks cast by local farmers and cost £280 of which the college contributed £120.

Memorials, especially to family members, were another source of reading rooms. The Redlynch reading room bears the inscription 'This Reading Room was erected in memory of William Taunton of Redlynch by his widow and children 1899'. Mrs. Starkey erected the reading room and coffee tavern at Rowde in 1887 in memory of her son, Rev. Andrew Starkey, who had become vicar of the parish in 1864 but died, aged only 33, in 1871. Canon King, vicar of Stratford-sub-Castle from 1849 to 1884, was remembered by the reading room erected by his widow, Mrs Mary King, a few years after his death. The Grittleton reading room was slightly different in that it was not a family memorial but was erected by public subscription in 1902 as a memorial to Rev. Henry Boldero, vicar of the parish for 36 years from 1864 to 1900.

It is not unusual to find public buildings erected to mark some royal occasion such as a coronation or anniversary. One might therefore have not been surprised to find Queen Victoria celebrated in such a way but there is no example of this in Wiltshire. There are, however, two memorial reading rooms in honour of George V – Upavon in 1911 to mark his coronation and Collingbourne Kingston in 1938 to commemorate his reign.

Finally, reading rooms might be erected by charitable trusts or organisations. When Mary Watney died in 1918 she left in her will a building, previously the village stores and telegraph office at All Cannings, to be used as a parish reading room. It also had a field nearby, the rent from which was used towards the maintenance of the reading room.

It might be asked why these various benefactors should wish to establish reading rooms rather than other village amenities. All the evidence suggests that the motives were genuinely altruistic – to improve the educational and recreational facilities for the men, particularly the young men, of the village. It might be suggested, also, that the close connection of the reading rooms with the temperance movement and as an alternative to the public house would indirectly benefit those who looked to employ men of the village.

The Buildings

Many of the earliest and most modest reading rooms were simply housed in a rented cottage or even in just one room. As the reading room was likely to be open only during the winter months, the cottage was rented for the season and another cottage used the following year. Perhaps it is not surprising that a lot of these failed after a relatively short existence and it is now extremely difficult to establish exactly where they were. The first reading room at Lacock, for example, was established in 1854 in Mrs. Newman's rooms for one quarter of the year. People at Mere were so anxious to get a reading room started that in 1883 they took Mrs. Rumsey's cottage next to the Talbot 'till better accommodation could be found', which in fact was achieved the next year. The reading rooms at Horningsham, Biddestone and Castle Combe all seem to have been in modest cottages with no substantial adaptations.

In other places a house or connected cottages were either bought or given. Significant alterations had to be undertaken to make the premises suitable to meet the requirements of a reading room which ideally needed a large room and a smaller one. In 1890 Sir Gabriel Gouldney purchased two cottages in the village street at Bradenstoke and gave these to the village. Various alterations and improvements were said to have been made to form two rooms, one for reading and writing and the other for games. At Warminster Sambourne Lord Bath agreed to lease two cottages to the vicar at a nominal rent for 21 years. Internal work was done to form a large room 35 feet by 14 feet which could be divided by a movable partition. The ceiling was lined with stained match boarding and the walls were also boarded to a height of 6 feet. Handsome free-stone windows were installed to give more light and a commodious porch was added.

Other types of building were also used. At Turleigh a club with reading room was only formed in 1920 following the gift by Major Scarth of a building which had been a brewery cellar and malt house but for many years was a stable, although it did have an attached cottage for the caretaker. At All Cannings the reading room was in the converted village stores and Telegraph Office. Until 1965 the cost of the upkeep of the room was met by the income from land surrounding it and in 1971 it became the village hall. A substantial conversion was undertaken in Norton Bavant . The village had used the parish hall as a reading room but this proved to be inconvenient and in 1895 they bought a workshop previously used by a carpenter and converted it at a cost of £15.

At least five reading rooms were in old school buildings. The one-classroom school at Chicklade opened in 1848 but closed by 1892 because of the decline in pupil numbers. It was then reported as being used as a reading room with an extra room as a vestry hall. There was a similar story at Chittoe where the school closed in 1906. The owner, Captain Spicer, then allowed the building to be used as an institute for men and boys replacing some previous accommodation. At Wroughton there appear to have been several changes of accommodation but in the 1890s a reading room and library was housed in the old Infants' school. The old school at Laverstock closed in 1888 and six years later a committee was formed to consider using it as a reading room. Approval was obtained from the Archdeacon: 'I know nothing which need prevent your using the Old School at Laverstock as a reading room. And I am glad to hear that there is a probability of its being turned in such good account'. A much earlier example was at Derry Hill where the old National School, built in 1843, was converted in 1873 to a Workman's Club and Institute containing not only a reading room but a library of nearly 800 books. The institute was strongly supported by the Marquess of Lansdowne and Lord Fitzmaurice and became a model for other reading rooms to be built on the Bowood estate.

Hotels and public houses were sometimes used especially where the Temperance movement had succeeded in getting rid of the licence to sell alcoholic drinks and had established a coffee tavern in its place. A good example of this was at Woodborough in 1891 when Lord Normanton, the owner of the Rose and Crown, withdrew the licence and then arranged for it to be carried on as a temperance hotel. Two rooms in the hotel were thrown together to make a room 29 feet long and 14 feet wide which was to be used as the village reading room. At Mere, part of the Angel hotel was sold off in 1883 and then leased to the Church Institute which comprised a Church club and a reading room. Basically this contained a large room for bagatelle and smoking, a smaller reading room and a committee room. There was also living accommodation for the manager who had three bedrooms upstairs, a room downstairs and the use of the kitchen. He paid a rent of £10 a year and provided refreshments, the profits from which he was allowed to keep. At Bratton the licensed premises known as the White Horse were converted to a coffee tavern in 1883. It was then said that it was likely the reading rooms, which occupied some rooms further along the lane, would move into the tavern but it is not certain whether this actually happened. In 1879 a new hotel was built in Bradford-on-Avon by Rev. Thring at the bottom of Horse Street on the site of the former White Hart. This was to be a temperance hotel with smoking and bagatelle rooms, a reading room and library. Upstairs were three bedrooms which were to be let to artisans and others requiring short term lodgings.

It was also not unusual to find the reading room housed in a wooden hut. During the First World War many army camps in Wiltshire were extended and new ones built. These largely consisted of wooden huts many of which were sold off after the war. These appeared in many guises, such as temporary additional accommodation for schools, and some villages bought them for their reading rooms. At Brinkworth in 1920 there were long discussions about how to provide better accommodation for their reading room. A site was acquired and at first it was intended to erect a new building of galvanised iron and wood. This plan was eventually abandoned and in its place they bought a wooden hut from the army camp at Chiseldon for £30 8s. This measured 60 feet by 20 feet and was erected on brick piers with a new corrugated iron roof. Staverton decided to build a new recreation and reading room in 1919 as a memorial to those who had fought in the war. It was perhaps appropriate therefore that they bought a wooden hut from the Red Cross hospital in Trowbridge and erected it on a site near the railway which they had leased from Victor Blake at the nominal sum of 1s. a year. Water and gas was laid on, a garden set out in front of the building and furniture bought at a total cost of £140. A year later a second Red Cross hut was acquired and equipped with a billiards table and a well stocked library. Similar wooden huts were erected at about the same time at Enford and Marden.

In the later Victorian age buildings of galvanised iron became very fashionable. They were relatively cheap, could be ordered 'off the peg' and coming in 'kit form' could be easily erected. Although they are perhaps most commonly associated with mission halls, they were also used in Wiltshire for a number of reading rooms. The reading room presented by Walter Powell M.P. to Little Somerford in about 1870 was described as being a wood and iron structure. It closed in the 1880s for lack of interest and was sold at auction in 1890 to Mr. Ponting of Malmesbury for £16. Another such building was erected at Oare in 1893 by Francis Rogers of Rainscombe. The main room, entered through a small porch, measured 25 feet by 13 feet. At right angles to this and joined by a movable partition was a smaller room 13 feet by 9 feet. An iron building of one large

Oare

room and a porch was erected at Purton Stoke in 1908 at a cost of £250. This was the result of efforts made by Miss Warrender and her friends and was originally opened as a Christian reading room. A much larger iron building was erected in Keevil in 1892. It was said to be capable of seating 300 and although described as the parish institute, it was probably more used for concerts and other entertainments. The cost of about £200 was met by Colonel Wallington with the site being given by Mr. Beach. It soon ran into financial difficulties and a sale of work and American fair was organised by Lady Hicks-Beach to liquidate the debt. At Fovant Rev. Earle purchased in 1886 at his own cost an iron building 40 feet by 20 feet and erected it on a site given by the Earl of Pembroke. Unfortunately it burnt down in 1908 and was replaced by another building which now serves as the village hall. A new reading room was opened in 1893 at Foxholes on a site given by the Marquess of Bath, mid-way between Longbridge Deverill and Crockerton both of which communities it was meant to serve. It was described as being 36 feet by 18 feet divided by folding doors into two compartments. Built of corrugated iron, it was lined with felt and matchboard, sized and varnished, to 'secure comfort and warmth'. The cost of the basic building was £92 but with various sundries and furniture the whole project came to just over £100. The very modest corrugated iron building erected at South Wraxall in 1903 as a church institute and reading room still exists. Finally there was a reading room of timber and corrugated iron on a brick foundation at Roundway.

A significant number of reading rooms had new, purpose built accommodation. In some cases they had started with modest, rented rooms but were sufficiently successful to be able to move on to much larger premises. At Potterne, for example, a Working Men's Social Club and Institute was opened in 1876 in a cottage near Mr. Stancomb's entrance lodge. This continued to flourish and by 1908 it had moved to newly built premises next to the school. Most frequently such a new building was paid for by a local benefactor or benefactors with help from other subscribers. Of the five reading rooms established by Lord

Lansdowne and Lord Fitzmaurice four were specially designed and erected between 1882 and 1884: Bremhill, Calstone Wellington, Foxham and Charlcutt. Bremhill, opened in 1882, was part of a major plan by Lord Lansdowne to improve the cottages on his estate and other facilities for his workers. The Foxham room was a substantial stone building 28 feet long by 18 feet broad. The walls were decorated with maps, portraits of Lord Fitzmaurice and also the grandfather of the then Lord Lansdowne. A clock presented by Lord Lansdowne occupied a prominent position in the room. Calstone Wellington was also opened in 1884 on a site previously occupied by a pair of cottages. It was of stone with red brick dressings and the interior was described as lofty with a very cheerful and comfortable appearance. It also had a photograph of Lord Fitzmaurice on the centre wall. The Great Somerford reading room established by Walter Powell in 1872 was a red-brick structure with arched windows, a high gabled roof and an ornate porch. A caretaker's house in a similar style was attached at one side. The Codford St. Mary reading room opened in 1893 was constructed of red brick, pointed black with Bath stone facings. It consisted of one large room 18 feet square and 12 feet high. Inside it had a matchwood dado 4 feet high all round the room and outside over the entrance were the initials of the founder A.B.(Alfred Blake). The new reading room at Corsley Heath was erected to a design (described as the Elizabethan rural style) by Mr. F. Brown, architect of Bath, and built by Mr. Ponton of Warminster. It was of red brick with a deep, sloping roof covered in French ornamental tiles. The arches over the door and window openings were formed with best Cattybrook red facing bricks. The room measured 39 feet by 24 feet and was divided by a panelled partition with sliding doors. There were two Leamington bar grates and ventilation was by one of Gibbs and Sons patent air-pump ventilators. The walls were stuccoed in dark grey, the ceiling plastered, the woodwork stained and varnished and the floor was of Kimberley's burnetized wood blocks laid diagonally. At Grittleton the reading room erected in 1902 was a quite ornate building in keeping with many other cottages in the village. The main reading room was single storey measuring 28 feet by 12 feet and could be divided into two equally sized rooms with a folding partition. At right angles was the two storey caretaker's house. On the ground floor was a living room, a scullery and a coal store with earth closets approached from the outside. Most oddly on the ground floor was another large room 18 feet by 12 feet and labelled 'Nurse's Room'. There was a somewhat similar position at East Kennett where the very substantial building erected in 1883 housed a reading room, a dispensary and a small hospital unit. Horningsham in the early 1890s had a reading room

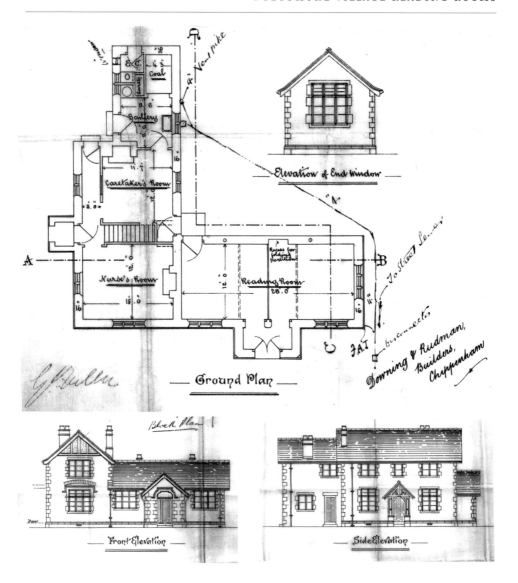

Grittleton: plans and elevations

in a cottage which almost certainly would have been provided by Lord Bath. In 1930 the then Lord Bath built a new village hall in memory of his late wife. This also contained a reading room and a billiard room and was remarkable for having been built largely from material salvaged from the gymnasium of the old Wiltshire Reformatory for Boys at Bugley near Warminster.

Some of the purpose-built buildings were quite extensive. The Workmen's Institute erected at Purton in 1879 by J.H.Sadler was built on the site of an old charity school. It contained a reading room, a large public room capable of seating 300 people and a tea and coffee room. There was also a cottage for the caretaker and the whole project cost about £3000. The Workman's Hall erected at Market Lavington in 1865 was another substantial building. It was of brick with giant pilasters, stone details, a large portico and particularly large sash windows on the first floor. The accommodation included a coffee room, a reading room and a small library. The reading room founded by Walter Powell at Malmesbury in 1870 had a frontage of 24 feet on Back Hill (now Silver Street) and ran for 170 feet to the rear. There were basically two rooms with, uniquely, the front room set aside for the use of the upper classes and the tradesmen with the inner room for the lower classes, although the partition could be removed to form one large room. The rooms were described as being decorated with a fine collection of buck and other horns, skins, etc. It also had accommodation for a caretaker with a sitting room and kitchen on the ground floor and a bedroom with water closet on the first floor. Underneath were coal cellars and underground passages.

Interiors

Reading rooms were designed to be comfortable, light and warm. It was hoped that this would help to recruit the working men whose normal accommodation was often cramped, overcrowded and in poor condition. Florence Nightingale put particular emphasis on the reading rooms being well lit and warm in contrast to the barracks in which the soldiers lived. An advocate of the reading room at Salisbury St. Martin's explained that working men wanted 'a bright fire, plenty of papers and books, if possible a room where talking might be allowed and a room for readers only, and a good cup of coffee and tea at so much a cup'.

The new reading room at Dilton Marsh, opened in 1880, was described as having a cheerful fire and lighted by lamps at night giving a cosy appearance especially when the blinds were drawn and the thick, red curtains stretched across the windows. The floor was covered with cocoa-nut matting and, perhaps uniquely, the walls were decorated with mottoes, the work of the Misses Phipps. These presented homely and moral messages such as 'Good works quench more than a bucket of water', 'As the labour, so the reward', 'Keep good men company and you shall be one of the number' and 'Do more than thou showest, speak less than thou knowest, lend more than thou browest'. In many of the rooms, the walls were panelled with matchwood, as at Codford and Heytesbury, or whitewashed but at Warminster Sambourne they were painted a rich salmon colour.

The walls were often decorated with various pictures and maps or with portraits of the benefactor who established the reading room. Paintings of Lord Fitzmaurice and Lord Lansdowne graced the walls of Foxham and Calstone Wellington while Holt had specially commissioned photographs (from Hellis and sons, Regent Street, London) of Mr. T.W.Forster, Major Forster, Alderman Beaven, Mr. F.T.Beaven, Mr. A. Mackay and Mr. E.C.Brown. A clock was usually placed in a prominent position.

Some inventories of furniture survive and these help to form a picture of what the rooms must have looked like. In 1890 Stratford-sub-Castle had 5 large tables, 1 small oak table, 3 small tables, 30 Windsor chairs, 1 cupboard, 2 book cases, 12 candle reflectors hung on the wall, 4 hanging oil lamps and reflectors and 4 reading lamps. Provision for catering was met with 24 cups and saucers, 12 tea spoons, 1 pair of sugar tongs, 24 soda glasses and a water bottle. The Codford room had a comfortable and cosy appearance, having two fireplaces and lighting from two oil lamps. Opposite the door was a handsome eight day clock, the gift of Mrs. Blake. Its furniture included four long tables, cupboards and ten benches with back rests. When Broughton Gifford reading room closed in 1937 the building was sold along with its contents – four deal tables (each 27in by 27in), 24 good lath-back chairs, other deal tables and a slow combustion stove.

But perhaps not all reading rooms were so well furnished and inviting. An article in The Academy in 1897 described what it called 'an ordinary reading room'.

> It is long and narrow. The floor is bare or partly covered with linoleum. The walls are whitewashed. There are a few pictures ... At one end of the room is a bagatelle board. The chairs are solid wood....On the mantelpiece are boxes of dominoes, draughts and chess. Above these is the library contained on two long shelves. The books are odd volumes of Chambers' Journal, two or three Waverley novels, Uncle Tom's Cabin, a volume of Sunday at Home and a score of other books mainly devotional.

Organisation

Management

Most reading rooms were managed by a President or Chairman, a Treasurer, a Secretary and an elected committee. Even when the room was established by a single benefactor, it was a deliberate policy to hand over the day to day running to the members in order to get their greater involvement. Lord Fitzmaurice made this clear when opening the Foxham reading room, stressing that he wished to interfere as little as possible. Very often the local vicar became chairman reflecting the real involvement of the church in establishing and maintaining the reading rooms. At Stratford-sub-Castle and at Lacock, for example, the chairman was always the vicar ex-officio.

Of the elected officials the key post and the most onerous one was that of secretary. Some served for many years and obviously the reading room came to depend on them. At Holt in 1894 there was a presentation to the secretary Mr. W. Moore in appreciation of many years of 'efficient and willing service'. Some £14 or £15 had been collected and Mr. Moore was given an illuminated address together with a gold chain and a Canterbury writing desk. At other times it was hard to find someone to undertake the job. At Pewsey in 1885 after the resignation of the secretary they could not get a replacement. Several gentlemen declined to serve until at last Mr. Deadman was induced to accept the office.

Some of the committees consisted of a mixture of the ordinary elected members and some of the more important men of the village. Teffont's committee had eight members – four trustees and four chosen at the general meeting. The committee to establish the reading room at Salisbury St. Martin's had five gentlemen and ten working men. Also, at Stratford-sub-Castle the committee had equal numbers of honorary members (those who paid a higher subscription) and ordinary members. There was greater control by the 'establishment' at Upavon where the small committee of five members consisted of the vicar and two churchwardens ex-officio and only two elected. Although there are many general comments about working men being on the committees, it is difficult to establish to what extent this was true. The one case at Mere, where we have information about the occupations of the committee members, there were no labourers but a private resident, the curate, a surveyor of highways, the registrar of births and deaths, a watch and clock maker and a draper/grocer/ironmonger.

There is little evidence about the elections and whether or not they were contested. But at Lacock, where there were six committee members elected half yearly, they did have a rather unusual procedure. Each member over 18 years of age was allowed to write down a list of six members and then deposit his ballot paper in a special box between 7 and 8.30 p.m. The vicar was responsible for opening the box, counting the votes and announcing the six who had received the most nominations. The only suggestion of problems and dissension occurred at Heytesbury in 1895. The proceedings at the A.G.M. were described as lively and there was adverse criticism of some of the actions of the committee although these were not identified. As a result the whole committee resigned; a fresh election was held and only one member of the old committee was re-elected.

In the larger reading rooms a manager or care-taker was appointed and sometimes accommodation was provided for him or her in or near the reading room. At Mere the manager also provided refreshments and was allowed to keep any profits which arose. In at

CHISELDON   READING-ROOM   AND
COFFEE TAVERN.
OPEN   DAILY

On Sundays from Opening till 10.30 a.m., 1 to 8.30 p.m.,
4.30 p.m. till Closing.

TARIFF, &c.

Large Cup of Tea	1½d.
Small Do.	1d.
Cup of Coffee	1d.
Cup of Cocoa	1d.
Slice of Bread and Butter	½d.
Slice of Bread and Marmalade	½d.
Slice of Cake	1d.
Bread and Cheese	2d.
Buns, Scones, Round Cakes	1d. and ½d.
Sheet of Paper, Envelope and Stamp	2d.

The Public are admitted to the Reading-Room on
payment of 1d. per day.

*Chiseldon:Refreshments advertisement (North Wilts
Herald February 1882)*

least two cases, Calstone Wellington and Derry Hill, women were appointed as the manager. Indeed at Derry Hill in 1897 Mrs. Hunt completed 23 years service and was presented with a purse containing £15 2s. She was then 80 years old.

The main issue for the committee was to decide the opening hours of the reading room. Many operated only during the winter months presumably because in the summer most labourers would be working during the long, light evenings. Porton was open from November to March. Tisbury closed at the end of the winter season on 24 April but authorised the secretary to close earlier than this 'in the event of good weather or other circumstances affecting the attendance'. The larger reading rooms were open for quite long periods; Lacock's hours were every day except Sunday from 9 a.m. to 9.30 p.m. Usually, however, the rooms were open for only a few nights a week and only in the evening. Fairly typical were Teffont (Tuesday, Wednesday, Friday 7 to 9.30 p.m.), Fonthill Gifford (Monday, Wednesday, Friday 6.30 to 9.30 p.m.) and Laverstock (Monday, Wednesday, Friday 7 to 10 p.m.). The hours were somewhat variable in other places. Erlestoke opened for three nights a week during winter from 7 to 9.30 p.m. except Saturdays when it closed at 9 p.m. and the six weeks before and after Christmas when it started half an hour earlier at 6.30. There was class distinction at Bremhill where the honorary members could come during the day but the ordinary members were excluded until 6 p.m. Without exception, the reading rooms did not open on Sundays.

Other rules had to be drawn up. The similarity of most of these suggests that there was some degree of copying from a neighbour. Procedures were necessary when more than one member wanted a particular newspaper. It was usually stipulated that a member could not keep a paper for more than 15 minutes (or ten minutes in some cases) after it had been requested by another member. Games could not be monopolised for more than three sets.

By the very nature of their foundation it was obvious that no intoxicating liquor was allowed in the reading rooms. Smoking was more debatable. Lacock and other places banned smoking altogether. Stratford-sub-Castle and Bremhill agreed to allow smoking although the vicar made it clear at Bremhill that he did not agree with this. In one case, at Bratton, there was a very contentious issue over whether or not the men could wear hats in the reading room. A letter in the Wiltshire Times for 6 January 1883 described how great an issue this was in the village and gave a lengthy and amusing description of the meeting which took place to make a decision. The party which wanted to make it compulsory for men to remove their hats managed to pack the committee with additional members so that in the end the committee had 60 members although the total membership of the reading room was only 63. When it was moved 'That any rule on the subject of wearing hats in a public room was unnecessary and that the matter should be left to personal inclination', the opponents broke forth with shouts of 'No discussion', 'No liberty' and 'Have a rule'. They then passed a rule which deprived them of exercising any discretion – and of being able to raise the issue on another occasion.

One might have expected the reading rooms to be orderly places and models of decorum. However, the need to make particular rules and some of the incidents which occurred suggest otherwise particularly with the younger members. At Ashton Keynes the first rule was 'All members must pay due respect to proper order and decorum, no whistling nor stamping of feet, swearing and bad language prohibited'. Chittoe specifically forbade bad language, spitting on floors and unruly behaviour. Indeed there was a complaint at Ashton Keynes that boys were in the habit of spitting on the coffee room floor and otherwise misbehaving themselves. Stratford-sub-Castle tried to avoid these problems by introducing a fine of 6d for each offence of bad language or improper conduct. Shaw held a special meeting in 1891 following a series of complaints about the behaviour of some youths and the vicar of Bremhill said that many of the older men did not go to the reading room because of the disorder which frequently prevailed there. To counteract this it became the normal practice for one of the committee men to be on duty each night in the room in order to ensure that order was kept. This was of little avail at Little Somerford in 1885 when Edwin Moore, the committee member, was assaulted by William Minty, a groom and drover, after he had been reprimanded for misconduct. Minty was brought before the Malmesbury magistrates and fined 24s.

Ashton Keynes was somewhat more liberal in its rules for they provided that if an intoxicated person came into the rooms and he behaved orderly he would be allowed to remain but if he was troublesome or noisy he would be asked to leave and, if necessary, turned out. But all the reading rooms were agreed in clearly stating they were 'neutral' in both politics and religion and any discussion on these topics was banned.

Other unforeseen problems arose, not always of the members' own making. A disastrous incident occurred at the Malmesbury reading room in 1881 when a bullock, being driven away from the market, broke loose and charged into the reading room. Attempts to get it out failed and in the meantime it destroyed chairs, upset tables and generally smashed up the furniture in both the reading room and the smoking room. After an hour it was eventually lassooed and dragged out by 20 men watched by a crowd of over 200.

Finance

Many of the smaller reading rooms existed on a very limited budget. Expenditure was mainly incurred on buying newspapers, heating, lighting and cleaning of the rooms. As this was virtually a fixed amount, the financial health of the institution depended on the members' subscriptions and any decrease in numbers could lead to a deficit. In the early days most of the reading rooms seemed to have just managed with a small balance each year. But very quickly some got into difficulties and ways had to be found to make good the shortfall each year. On the other hand, the very large reading rooms/workmen's institutes had a substantial turnover.

In 1889 Heytesbury had an income from subscriptions of £4 18s 4d and an expenditure of £4 12s 7d. Stratford-sub-Castle, despite its new, purpose-built building, was also a relatively small organisation. Its income in 1886-7 was only £10 4s 10d but its expenditure was £11 15s 11d although this included the special cost of £2 10s for repairing the roof. In 1888-9 they were still recording a balance of £2 7s. but decline set in soon after this. Lacock was opened in 1854 but it was sufficiently well endowed to be able to abolish subscriptions in 1856. That year they started with a balance of £10 17s 2d and their only additional income was £1 14s 3d from a lecture and £2 19s from the sale of old papers. Their expenditure of £6 18s 2d included rent £1 5s, newspapers £2 9s, coal 5s.10d, candles 5s 4d and a one-off payment for a bookcase and varnishing it £2 3s. Corsley did particularly well with an income in 1895 of £14 3s 3d and an expenditure of only £3 16s but this was only because the cost of newspapers and of the caretaker was met by Mr. Cookson.

Hilmarton faced substantial deficits in 1897 and 1898. Their income was about £10 to £12 but their expenditure was double this. They were fortunate that the difference, £11 6s 5d in 1897 and £13 13s 6d in 1898, was made up by Sir John Poynder, M.P. However, in 1899 he said it was time for the reading room to be self-supporting. A new committee was formed and they were so successful in raising income that they had a balance of nearly £5 at the end of the year. Ashton Keynes also had a deficit in 1892 of £2 to £3 and this was paid by Mr. Milling. Bromham had to look to benefactors to balance their accounts for 1913 and 1914 with contributions of 5s from the vicar and 14s 7d from the Temperance Society. It was, in fact, in the period of the First World War and soon afterwards that many reading rooms faced financial difficulties and had to find new ways of making ends meet. Bremhill faced its first, relatively small deficit in 1919 which was immediately wiped out by the members present. Later they had to make up a larger amount of £1 8s 11d and the vicar proposed to raise this sum by arranging some kind of amusement and to hold a whist drive charging 1s 6d for admission. Fonthill Bishop in 1928 very much depended on the receipts from the use of the billiard table which produced £5 15s 9d out of its total income of £14 1s 9d. Only £2 15s came from members' subscriptions while donations totalled £4. Charlcutt was luckier in that by 1928 it had a capital sum of £400 invested in 4% stock although it is not clear how this accumulated. Interest on this amounted to half their annual income and more than covered their expenditure.

In a large institution such as Highworth the budget was on a much bigger scale. In 1879 they had an income of £126 1s 5d and an expenditure of only £66 8s 9d. Subscriptions produced £70 but only £18 of this came from working men at 6d a month; the remaining £52 came from 50 subscribers. The sale of coffee, cocoa and biscuits made a profit of £28 15s. By 1884 receipts for the year had increased to £361 19s 8d but expenditure had risen more rapidly to £319 16s 6d.

Redlynch; the tea room. (Reproduced by courtesy of the Peter Daniels Archive)

Membership

As the whole raison d'être of the reading rooms was to keep men off the streets and away from the public houses, it is understandable that in the majority of cases membership was restricted to males. There was usually a debate about the minimum age with the concern that if children were admitted it would deter others. The vicar of Longbridge Deverill, for example, expressed his opinion that if boys were to be admitted he was afraid the room would not be what they wished to see it. The most frequent minimum age was 16 but in Bromham no one under 18 was admitted. In other cases it was lower with 15 at Chittoe, Longbridge Deverill and Oare and 14 at Bremhill and Erlestoke. At Stratford-sub-Castle the basic age was 16 but exceptions could be made by a special decision of the committee so that in 1886 James Williams and Edmund Tryhorn, both under 16, were admitted. As the reading rooms developed there were cases where the original minimum age was reduced possibly to increase numbers or through the wish to influence boys at an early age. In 1887 Ashton Keynes reduced its age from 16 to 14 and in 1899 Laverstock brought the age down to 13.

It is very difficult to establish what proportion of the members of any particular reading room were labourers and how many were tradesmen or professional people. There is some indication at Ashton Keynes which had a particularly large membership and where labourers paid 1d a week and tradesmen and others 2d a week. In 1884-5 61 paid 1d and 73 paid 2d. The first list includes at least 13 agricultural labourers, two general labourers, two factory labourers, a groom and a gardener. The second list has only three farmers and is heavily dominated by craftsmen notably cordwainers, carpenters and masons. The tradesmen are represented by three butchers and a baker. Some of the young members appear to have been below the official minimum age of 17 but almost all are the sons of existing members whether labourers or tradesmen. From this evidence it does appear that the Ashton Keynes reading room attracted the working class which the movement was aimed at. They also had an impressive list of 19 honorary members, each paying between 10s and £1 1s a year, which included the Duke of Cleveland (who bought the Ashton Keynes estate in 1848),

Sir Daniel Gooch M.P., Captain Salmon, Captain Dickenson and Mr. Story Maskelyne. In 1880 Highworth had 105 members of which about half were said to be working men.

There are some rare examples where women were also admitted. At Mere in 1885 females could become members at a fee of 1s 6d a quarter or 5s a year and six ladies were accepted that year. There also seem to have been female members at Ashton Keynes. But in both cases there were restrictions especially that all females were excluded from the rooms after 5 p.m. Hilmarton had its first female members in 1898 – Mrs. Perry, Mrs. C. Smith and Mrs. Wiltshire. Ladies were involved in the establishment of some reading rooms such as Miss Livingstone, the vicar's daughter, at Brinkworth and Lady Doreen Long at West Ashton. The general attitude was, as so ungallantly expressed by the vicar of Seend, that the room was open to men only but there was nothing to prevent members of the 'fair sex' from supporting it financially.

The village reading room was specifically founded for the benefit of the local community and usually membership was restricted to that area. The Porton Reading and Recreation Room, for example, was open only to men resident in the parish of Idmiston which included the hamlets of Porton and Gomeldon. The parish of Longbridge Deverill included the hamlet of Crockerton and the reading room was deliberately built at Foxholes mid way between the two communities. Provision was almost always made, however, for members to introduce visitors on payment of 1d a night. Ashton Keynes maintained a register of such visitors who came from a surprisingly wide range of places, perhaps reflecting a much greater movement of people than one might have expected at that period. Relatively local places such as New Swindon, Brinkworth and Chippenham might not be considered exceptional but the list also included Cheltenham, Cirencester, Stroud, Bloxham, Llandudno, London, Gloucester, Bristol, Kettering and Newport (Mon.). Various reading rooms showed differing attitudes to outsiders. When the reading room at East Knoyle was re-opened in 1889 it was said to have been attended by many of the workmen who had come into the area to work on the re-building of Clouds after its disastrous fire. These were apparently very pleased to have a large, comfortable room in which to spend their evenings. This contrasts with the position at All Cannings. An article in The Builder in 1872 reported that much new building was taking place in the area with workmen from outside the area. These were, however, denied access to the newly opened reading room so 'with all the talk about the difficulty of weaning men from the public house or beer shop and getting them to spend their leisure time in a better way, they have in many instances only Hobson's Choice'. There was no disagreement, however, about making the reading rooms available to soldiers during the First World War. Tisbury particularly welcomed men from the South Western Mounted Brigade and later also allowed the use of the room by soldiers at the military hospitals in the area. Urchfont was popular with the Canadian soldiers based on Salisbury Plain. In 1900 the Navvy Mission Society organised a large hut at Bulford for the navvies and carpenters working on the extension of the camp there. On Sundays there was a Bible class and evensong, on Thursdays an entertainment and on other nights it was used as a reading and recreation room.

One or two reading rooms were completely free because of generous contributions from local benefactors. Most, however, charged a modest fee in order to try to make the reading room self-supporting. This worked out, on average, at about 1d a week but there was a wide variety of scales partly because the rooms were open for varying lengths of time during the year. Dilton Marsh and Chittoe, for example, charged 1s. a quarter while Stratford-sub-Castle charged 1s for the period from the start of the winter season to the end of December and 1s for the period from January to the Spring closure. Sometimes an entrance fee was levied on new members such as 6d at Laverstock and 2s.6d at Upavon. It is particularly interesting to note that there was often a differentiation in fees. At Ashton Keynes, as mentioned above, tradesmen were charged 2d a week but labourers only 1d a week. There was a similar arrangement at Lacock where farmers and tradesmen paid an entrance fee of 2s plus 2d a week while labourers paid 6d entrance and 1d a week. Manton charged less for the younger members; 4d a month for the 14 to 16 year olds compared with 6d for adults. All the reading rooms also had what they called 'Honorary members' who paid at least 10s a year (or 5s at Oare). They may have had special privileges as at Bremhill but basically this seems to have been a way of raising money from the more affluent people of the village.

The reading rooms varied greatly in their size and number of members and this was not particularly related to the size of the village. Some started with great enthusiasm, managed to maintain the momentum and saw a steady increase in their numbers. Others very quickly withered and closed.

Some of the largest were at Derry Hill with 110 members in 1875, Holt with about 100 in 1896 and Salisbury St. Martin's (not strictly a village) with 177 ordinary members when it opened in 1876. Ashton Keynes is a good example of an early decline after a very impressive start. Members paid weekly and by

November the numbers had built up to 122 and then declined towards the end of the season giving an average of 76 for the winter months. The following year they had only 50 in November declining to 20 by the summer. Then in 1901-2 the total number of members had dropped to 38 with an average attendance of only 25. Stratford-sub-Castle in 1886-7 had 29 members for the first half of the season and 28 in the second half. But by 1892 they had only 8 ordinary and 12 honorary members with the highest attendance on any one night of 9 and the lowest 0. Numbers picked up slightly the next year with 12 ordinary members enrolled by Christmas. Heytesbury seems to have managed an increasing number with 38 members in 1884 but 19 quarterly and 50 weekly members in the next year. Most commonly the reading rooms were quite small with between 20 and 30 members – Oare (25), Lacock (22) and Berwick St. James (31).

Reading and Recreation

Reading and recreation were the two central activities of the new rooms but, although many of the founders clearly favoured the educational value of reading, recreation seems to have been the greater attraction especially for the young men.

Newspapers

The essential provision of every reading room was the supply of a number of newspapers and periodicals. Detailed information on what was available has survived for eight of the county's reading rooms. One of the earliest of the county's reading rooms at Lacock had a rather limited range of papers in 1854. It had only the *Times* and the *Devizes Gazette* together with the *Illustrated London News*, *Punch* and *Household Words*. The later reading rooms tended to have a much wider choice not least because of the larger number of daily newspapers which became available in the second half of the 19th century. The widest selection by far was at Mere. In 1884 they had two daily national papers, the *Daily News* and the *Standard* plus the local papers *Western Gazette*, *Salisbury Journal* and *Frome Times*. In addition they took a strange mixture of *Field*, *Builder*, *Punch*, *Church of England Chronicle*, *Pictorial World*, *Penny Illustrated*, *English Mechanic*, *British Workman*, *Quiver*, *Chambers Journal*, *Funny Folks* and *Church Banner*. Various members also lent *Illustrated London News*, *Church Bells*, *Boys Own Paper* and *Penny Post*. A year later they decided to take *Whitaker's Almanac* and *Evening Standard*. Porton also agreed on a wide range when the reading room opened in 1907: *Daily Graphic*, *Daily Telegraph*, *Daily News*, *Daily Mirror* and *Daily Express* plus the local papers *Salisbury Journal*, *Salisbury Times* and *Salisbury Mirror*. In 1908 they replaced the *Telegraph* with *Gardening*. Stratford-sub-Castle paid for only two publications when it opened in 1886, *Daily Telegraph* and *Illustrated London News*. But generous members, especially the Chairman and the Secretary, promised the daily and weekly papers *Morning Post*, *Standard*, *Times*, *Graphic*, *Salisbury Journal* and *Western Gazette* and the periodicals *Turner*

Magazine, Punch, Gardener, Bee Journal, Good Words and *Sunday Magazine*. Even the small village of Chittoe had access to *Daily Mirror, Daily Mail, Daily Express, Daily News* and *Wiltshire Gazette* and *Wiltshire Times*. The wide range at Bromham in 1912, *Daily Chronicle, Daily News, Daily Mail and Daily Mirror,* had to be reduced in 1914 because of financial difficulties and only the *Daily Mail* and *Daily Chronicle* were retained.

It must be remembered that in the 19th century most national and local newspapers had a strong political bias even compared with those of today. Reading room committees seemed to have been anxious to have a sufficient range of newspapers to give different views on the great issues of the day. Lord Fitzmaurice, on opening the Calstone Wellington reading room in 1884, praised the neighbouring village of Foxham which had decided to take one Liberal daily, one Conservative daily, one weekly Liberal and one weekly Conservative. As most reading rooms professed to have no political or religious bias, this matter of what papers to take was obviously an important one. At Purton in 1880, for example, there was great objection to the committee's proposal to dispense with the *Telegraph*. The members thought it essential to be able to read both sides in political affairs and the *Daily News* was considered to be so pronounced in views to one side that those who differed had no alternative to read.

A great fuss also occurred at Market Lavington in 1885. A contentious, radical newspaper *The Democrat* appeared in the reading room although it is not clear whether it was purchased by the committee or simply introduced by a member. Several of the principal members threatened to resign unless it was removed while another member, a near relative of the editor of 'this mischievous print', stoutly opposed its discontinuance.

Some interesting light is shed on the actual provision and delivery of newspapers. In 1885 Mr. Gleed, secretary of the Ashton Keynes reading room, was in correspondence with the W.H.Smith newspaper stall on Swindon station. He eventually arranged for the papers to be sent by the 9.05 a.m. train to Minety Station, some three miles away, from which they would be collected. Gleed also said that only six daily papers were taken in the village and he tried to arrange for these to be parcelled together with those for the reading room. Lacock had some difficulty over their paper suppliers. In 1857 they replaced Marshall and Co. with Noyes (possibly of Chippenham). Although the terms were the same, Noyes agreed to throw in a free Bristol paper weekly. A local man, Moore, was employed to collect the papers but he proved unsatisfactory and was replaced by Joseph Jones. He doesn't seem to have been much better and his application for an increase in salary was turned down. Within the reading room a junior member, James Webb, was given free admittance in return for keeping the *Times* and other papers in good order.

It was normal practice to sell off old newspapers and magazines and the income from this was a welcome addition to the annual budget. Lacock was fairly typical in its rule that at 8 o'clock every Monday evening, all weekly papers would be sold if six days old and all daily papers if three days old.

Libraries

It was the ambition of many reading room committees to add a library to their other facilities although very few seem to have achieved this. At Fosbury, Shalbourne and Yatesbury there appear to have been village libraries but probably not a reading room associated with them. Kelly's Directory reports a free lending library at Fosbury with 500 volumes in 1911 and 400 volumes in 1927. The Shalbourne library was more tenuous, Thomas Kingston erected a school there in 1856 but it closed in 1873. When he died in 1903 he left money to establish a charity with two sections – Library branch and Exhibitions branch. The old school was to be used for the advancement of the education of the children of labourers, cottagers and other poor persons together with adults by means of a library to be called Thomas Kingston's library. In 1905 it was reported that the building was in need of considerable repair and nothing had been done to carry out the scheme. But the last vicar, Rev. Shuttleworth, had left a small library of 250 books in charge of Mr. Morris, master of the elementary school, and it was hoped that this might form the foundation of the proposed library. Yatesbury was recorded in 1883 as having a free library of about 250 volumes. It had then been in existence for five years and it was 'really wonderful how the books are read'.

There are firm references to reading rooms with a library at Ashton Keynes, Highworth, Hilmarton, Lacock, Mere, Stratford-sub-Castle and Tisbury. By far the largest was that at Stratford-sub-Castle which in 1886 had 386 books plus a number of unbound periodicals and papers (see appendix). It is not known how these were acquired but it is most likely that they were given by various people in the village. Highworth already had 150 volumes by 1880 as did Hilmarton in 1890. The new reading room opened at Mere in 1884 and two years later they decided to add a library. They had a number of gifts including 50 volumes from Rev. Wyld but they also bought a number, mostly secondhand, from Brown and Co. booksellers at Salisbury. The accounts show donations of £12 7s. which they spent on books (£5 12s 6d), binding books (£3 2s 3d), a book case (£3 7s 6d) and shelves and steps (13s and 5s). The Ashton Keynes library was also composed of donated books – 58 from Captain Salmon with further lists from Mr. Broad and Mrs. Wilkins. Steeple Ashton was successful in 1888 in obtaining a grant from the London based Rebecca Hussey book charity. A list of books valued £4 (equivalent to £5 4s at publisher's prices) was approved provided Steeple Ashton contributed £2. The reading room at Lacock had a very early library and the records show the committee spending £6 9s on about 30 books in 1855. The Tisbury example is particularly interesting. The institute was opened in 1913 as a 'Library and Reading Room' although by 1916 it was much more used by children than adults. But in the 1920s there started a connection with the County Librarian which eventually led to the establishment of a full branch of the County Library. In 1925 he agreed to supply Tisbury with 150 volumes which he promised to exchange every six months. By 1934 the library had 100 adult and 58 junior members with 1108 books issued in one year. The library became a full branch of the county library in the 1950s.

It is difficult to see any firm plan about what books to have in the library largely, perhaps, because so many of the books were donated and you got what you were given. The committees did, however, exercise some control over what was in the library and no new books could be introduced without their approval. Some broad categories can be identified such as history, natural history, travel and exploration and 'good works' but there was also a good proportion of fiction and some books obviously aimed for younger children. Hume's *History of England* vols 1 – 8, Smollett's *History of Ireland* vols 1 – 5, *Life of Gladstone, Last days of Pompeii*, and *Stories of Old England* represented serious historical works and but one wonders to what extent they appealed to the young labourers of the village. The Victorian interest in exploration, adventure and the 'Empire' was also reflected in many of the books. *The Cannibal Islands, My First Voyage to Southern Seas, Famous discoveries by sea and land, Letters from Sarawak* and *Voyage around the World* might have created greater excitement. Natural history included some books which are now regarded as 'classics' such as *Natural History of Selborne* and Wood's *Natural History of Birds and Animals* together with more general works *British Butterflies* and *Home Naturalist*. Religious works always formed a large section of any Victorian library and the reading rooms were no exception. Thus we find a whole range with such intriguing titles as *Plain Sunday Reading for Farm Boys, Doing and Suffering, Lectures on the Pilgrims Progress, Can you die in peace?* and inevitably *Household Words* and *Sunday at Home*.

Fiction featured quite largely with what we now regard as 'classics' – *Robinson Crusoe, Waverley Novels, Little Women, Adam Bede, Mill on the Floss* and *Uncle Tom's Cabin*. Not surprisingly, Dickens appears frequently with, for example, Steeple Ashton having copies of *Pickwick Papers, Nicholas Nickleby, David Copperfield, Oliver Twist, Dombey and Son, Martin Chuzzlewit, Old Curiosity Shop, Barnaby Rudge* and *The Tale of Two Cities*. One is reminded that at the time the reading rooms were flourishing Dickens was a contemporary novelist; Lacock in 1854 decided to buy the monthly instalments of *Little Dorritt* as they were published. Children were also catered for. Steeple Ashton had *Swiss Family Robinson* and the lesser known *Froggy's Little Brother* while Stratford-sub-Castle included *Beeton's Boys Annual, Our Nursery Picture Book* and two volumes of *Fairy Tales*.

Unlike newspapers which could not be taken out of the reading room, the libraries were lending libraries with rules and arrangements for the issue of books. At Lacock, the secretary was in attendance every Monday evening to issue books. Only members could borrow books and if any member was found lending a book to a non-subscriber, he was fined 1s. Books could be kept no longer than two weeks with a fine of 1d a week for late returns. There was a similar arrangement at Mere with an appointed librarian, Arthur Norris, who was to be present on Thursday evenings from 7 to 7.30 and Monday mornings 12.30 to 1.0. At Stratford-sub-Castle members could borrow only one book at a time but could keep it for up to four weeks.

Games

The provision of a range of games was a vital attraction for the young men of the village. The most important and popular of these was bagatelle. This took various forms but was quite different from what we now recognise as bagatelle. It was very much like billiards being played on a similar table with cues but with a number of cups towards the end of the table rather than pockets around the sides. Billiards was more uncommon but does appear rather later in some reading rooms. In 1894 the Holt reading room was especially extended to provide a billiard room. Heytesbury, Fonthill Bishop and Fonthill Gifford (where members were charged 2d a game) also had billiard tables in the 1920s. Mere also charged for bagatelle – the loser to pay 1d if only two played but, if more than two players, each loser paid ½d.

Chess, draughts, dominoes, ring-board and darts were usually found in the rooms and, at Chiseldon, 'other innocent games'. Cards were generally allowed, especially for whist, but were expressly banned at Mere. Whatever the game, gambling or any playing for money was strictly forbidden. Porton was given some board games – 'Alma' (probably Halma) and 'Reverse' (probably Reversi, a board game similar to draughts which was introduced in the late 19th century).

Activities

When the reading rooms started, their activities were largely for individuals, especially reading with some small groups for games of bagatelle and cards. But quite quickly they developed wider activities involving most members and transforming the reading room into something like a social club. The earliest and most common of these activities was a concert which was also aimed at raising funds for the reading room. In fact concerts and smoking concerts were often held in order to raise sufficient money to establish a reading room in the village. Mostly these were relatively simple affairs with a series of songs performed by members of the reading room. The number of people attending could, even so, be large and the entertainment would then be held in the schoolroom where there would have been more space. Great trouble was taken to ensure that the evening would be enjoyed. At Corsley in 1894, for example, the front and rear of the platform was decorated by collections of exotic flowers from the Sturford Mead conservatories and arranged by their gardener, Mr. Thomas. In some places it was possible to use outside entertainers such as the Bourne Valley Brass Band at Porton in 1909. But Porton also had a weekly concert for members only. This followed the purchase of a piano which was also hired out to other groups using the room.

Dances were less common but did appear in some places especially after 1900. At Derry Hill a very successful dance was held in 1910 with dancing kept up until after two in the morning to the music of a piano, violin and cornet. Holt also held an annual soiree and dance with over 100 attending.

The other common activity was an annual tea or dinner often linked with the reading room's annual general meeting. Corsley, Berwick St. James and Farley all held annual dinners in the 1890s with about 50 to 60 people attending. At other places such as Hilmarton they had an annual tea rather than a dinner. But these occasions could be held on a much grander scale. At Holt in 1875 the friends of the reading room gave a public tea to the working men, young and old, with their wives and sweethearts. This was held in a tent in the orchard adjoining the reading room and some 300 attended. At Market Lavington 76 sat down to a vegetarian supper in 1886 to celebrate the 21st anniversary of the opening of the Workmen's Hall. There were four courses. First, roast potatoes and mashed potatoes; second, apple, gooseberry and cherry pies, baked milk puddings from a mixture of half rice and half pearl barley; then tarts, cheese, butter, biscuits and whole meal bread; lastly oranges, apples and filberts. Water was the only beverage. It was reported that 'this novel repast was much enjoyed'. There was a tea on a similar scale at Stratford-sub-Castle in 1888 when for 60 people they provided 50lbs of plum cake (although a later note suggested 40lbs would have been enough), 3 gallons of tinned bread (i.e. baked in tins), 3 lbs of fresh butter, 8 lbs loaf sugar, 1½ lbs tea and 1¾ gallons of milk.

It was perhaps not surprising to see the recreational and sporting activities developing into matches against neighbouring reading rooms. In 1894 a group of reading rooms in the Warminster area (Codford, Heytesbury, Horningsham, Maiden Bradley) played a series of games against each other. The results of all these matches were reported in the local press. The usual games were bagatelle and draughts but in the match between Market Lavington and West Lavington crib and whist were also included. In the Pewsey area in 1910 there was a much more formal Challenge Shield competition which comprised whist, single cribbage, dominoes and rings (this being substituted for draughts). The formal meeting to make the arrangements was held at the Greyhound Hotel in Pewsey with representatives from Hilcott, Milton, Oare and Woodborough.

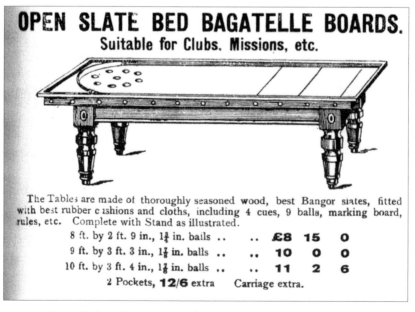

Bagatelle board (Gamages Christmas Bazaar Catalogue 1913)

They also sent out an invitation to Honey Street to join them. They claimed that this new competition had stimulated interest in the reading rooms. An internal tournament between two teams involving French bagatelle, cannon and draughts was organised by Mr. Drew and Mr. Hurn at Rowde in 1897. The object of the match was to play for a tea with the winners paying 3d each and the losers 9d. After an even struggle Mr. Drew's team won by two points.

Some reading rooms went further and formed their own cricket team; Stratford-sub-Castle in 1887 and Mere in conjunction with the Temperance Society in 1884 (charging members 6d a session). When the Easton Royal reading room opened in 1895 they decided to form a cricket team to occupy the summer months when the reading room was not open. Wootton Bassett did not actually have its own team but had a close association with the Red Star football team which was allowed to use its rooms for meetings. Perhaps most important of all was the formation of the Rifle Club at Porton in 1912. It was allowed to use the reading room two nights a week from 8 to 9.30. Members paid an entrance fee of 6d and had to be over 17 (later reduced to 16). Air rifles were used and members had 15 shots a penny for practice. When the reading room ran into trouble in 1915 with a decline in numbers, it was acknowledged that it could not pay its way without the income from the rifle club. Derry Hill was unique in having a Fife and Drum band. This was resurrected in 1882 and was sufficiently flourishing by 1885 to decide to have its own uniform consisting simply of a special cap of the Coldstream Guards pattern. The band raised 30s and, with other contributions, this was enough to buy 17 caps.

More intellectual activities were also organised but these tended to be less popular than the sporting occasions. The most common was a lecture. At Atworth in 1879 Rev. Sainsbury, the vicar, gave a lecture on 'Journey and voyage of St. Paul, especially Cyprus' illustrated by colour diagrams. The press commented 'Such lectures were never heard in Atworth before; but now the right man is come to the right place, it is hoped he will be spared for many long years to minister to us'. Rev. Swayne's address at Heytesbury on his recent tour of Jamaica in 1896 was well attended although perhaps it demanded some degree of stamina from the audience as it lasted for two hours. In 1856 Rev. Wilkinson gave a lecture on 'Stonehenge'; members were free, others paid 6d for a front seat or 2d for a back seat. Wylye opened its season in 1890 with a 'dioramic entertainment' given by Mr. Baker of Salisbury, starting with photographs of great cathedrals and other buildings including Wilton. A more literary topic was chosen at Lacock in 1876 when Rev. Darby of Bath lectured on 'The Life and Genius of Edgar Allen Poe'.

Unfortunately the evening was very dark and dirty and consequently there was a small attendance. With the close connection between the reading rooms and the temperance movement it was inevitable that some topics would be about drinking and health. Highworth in 1878 was addressed by Mr. Hodgson Pratt, chairman of the Working Men's Club and Institute in London. He ventured to submit that, although several remedies were now proposed as a cure for drunkenness, none was so effectual as the establishment of an institute in every village and town in the country. Men could go there to spend hours of their leisure time in healthy as well as necessary recreation, in reading papers and improving their mind 'without being obliged to resort to low, degrading and often immoral associations connected with a public house.' A more general lecture on 'Health' was given by Mr. Samuel Saunders at the annual meeting at Market Lavington in 1885. He maintained that the great error of the present day was too luxurious living with those who could afford it and the attempt among the poorer classes to live upon fine bread instead of bread and porridge made from the whole of the grain. He also criticised the indulgence in tea, tobacco and alcohol. This was followed by a coffee supper and a lively conversation until 10 p.m. Holt formed a debating society in 1896 and the first topic was 'Is smoking injurious?' Mr. Green proposed the motion and Mr. House opposed it. There was an animated discussion and the final vote was 17 for the motion and 19 against. However, the society did not flourish and had been abandoned by 1898.

In the early 20th century there was a move by Local Education Authorities to establish domestic science centres where the older girls from the local elementary schools could have lessons in cookery, laundry work, etc. Authority was obtained from the Department of Education to hold these in some reading rooms, in particular Cherhill, Great Bedwyn, Lydiard Millicent, Teffont and Urchfont.

There are a few examples of club outings. In 1901 Derry Hill went to Bournemouth and the next year they combined with Charlcutt, Foxham and Calstone in an excursion to Dawlish and Teignmouth. On both occasions Lord Lansdowne and Lord Fitzmaurice contributed £10 towards the cost. Fonthill Bishop also had annual outings although this was not until the 1930s. In 1933 they went to the Tidworth Tattoo in a 20 seater bus with each member paying 6d. The following year (and again in 1938) they went to Portsmouth again in a 20 seater bus. They took with them their own refreshments: 5 lbs cooked ham, 4 lbs cheese, 1 lb butter, 3 gallons of beer, 1 gallon of cider, 1 dozen minerals and five 4 lb loaves of bread.

Decline

It is much more difficult to chart the decline of the reading rooms simply because a closure would not be either newsworthy or something which a village would want to herald in the same way as the opening of a new room. Certainly all the reading rooms, as such, had closed by the start of the Second World War. The picture is slightly confused by some village halls still using the name 'Reading Room' although the original function had long ceased. Chilmark, East Grimstead, Corsley, Stratford-sub-Castle and Corston are but some examples of this practice.

Many of the smaller reading rooms must have been very short lived and, as they were most likely to have been in a rented room or cottage, they have left no physical evidence of their ever having existed. For some villages there are just one or two references in the 19th century to reading rooms and virtually no further information. There are simply single entries in Kelly's Directory for Goatacre (1890), Marston Meysey (1885) and Southwick (1895) while Upton Lovell, Avebury and Westwood just have passing mention in the local press.

It is quite common to find that the initial enthusiasm was difficult to maintain and numbers fairly quickly tailed off with the consequent financial crisis this caused. At Stratford-sub-Castle, for example, the initial membership of about 30 when the room opened in 1886 had dwindled to under 10 in 1892. In other cases the decline in membership necessitated a special meeting to decide whether to continue or not. Holt had opened in 1873 but closed by 1881 and then became a wool store. A successful revival took place in 1885 and the reading room then thrived with a billiard room being added in 1894. Undoubtedly the First World War had a great impact on the village reading rooms. Firstly, a large number of the young men for whom the reading room was mainly intended were away in the armed forces, then the high casualty rate in the war seriously reduced the number of men in most villages. Bromham had 48 paid up members in 1912 but this number had dropped to 16 in 1919 making the coffee tavern and reading room unviable. In some places such as Codford and Tisbury, numbers were temporarily increased during the war by allowing soldiers who were barracked locally to use the reading room. But as these were given free use, the financial problems remained. One might have expected some kind of revival after the war and certainly a few new reading rooms were opened in the 1920s but this was very limited and the general decline continued.

Bremhill is a well documented example of this sort of decline, the attempts which were made to remedy it and the ultimate failure. The establishment of the room by Lord Fitzmaurice in 1882 was greeted with great enthusiasm and 200 attended the opening ceremony of a public tea, speeches and music. But at the annual meeting in 1912 only seven members were present. The number of members continued to decline and action had to be taken to remedy the annual deficit such as cancelling some papers and increasing the subscriptions. In 1921 the committee, after seeking the advice of Lord Fitzmaurice, all resigned and a new start was attempted. This enabled the reading room to stagger on for a few more years but in January 1924 there was a much larger deficit especially because of the increased cost of papers and fuel. It was then decided to close the reading room.

The starting point for the reading rooms had been the creation of a warm, comfortable environment in contrast to the very poor, overcrowded condition of most labourers' cottages. Improvements began to be made to many of these cottages in the early 20th century and more generally so in the 1920s. This would mean that there was less incentive to go out in the winter evenings. As daily newspapers became more numerous and cheaper, it was much more likely that they would be purchased by individual workmen rather than their having to go to a communal room to get access to them.

Some villages were just unlucky. The reading rooms at Great Somerford and Little Somerford had been established by Walter Powell but they remained in his ownership and, when he died in 1882, there was no special provision in his will and the rooms were sold by his executors.

A fairly typical transition was for the social and communal activities of the reading room to become less popular and the concept of membership of a man's club was replaced by a room which could be hired out to a variety of organisations for their separate activities. An indication of this trend is the report from Fonthill Gifford in 1934 that they had managed to play all their billiards matches but it was difficult to raise a team. The most natural move was therefore for the reading room to become the village hall or to be used for some other community purpose. Of the 54 reading room buildings which can still be traced in Wiltshire, 24 are still used as village halls. In other cases such as East Grimstead and Staverton, the original reading room building has been replaced in recent years on the same site by a larger, more substantial building. The move from reading room to village hall can be clearly traced in Durrington. A reading room was developed in the old schoolroom in 1912. By the 1920s it was too small for the expanding population of the village. A new village hall was then built, the old reading room being sold and the proceeds going towards the new facility. Six have some other form of community use.

After closure, some reading rooms were sold and converted into private houses or business premises. 24 examples have been traced in the county including Codford, Broughton Gifford, Grittleton, East Kennett, Manton and Redlynch. In some cases the original building has been so modified and enlarged that it is difficult to identify the original core reading room but often a date stone or dedication has been preserved. Sometimes the present name of a house is the only tangible reminder of the existence of a reading room in that village.

The reading rooms at Purton, Market Lavington and Tisbury are now libraries/museums while the Young Farmers Club have their base in the old Purton Stoke room. Of Walter Powell's foundations, that at Great Somerford has been converted into a Methodist chapel and the Malmesbury rooms are used for a children's nursery.

Was the village reading room movement a success? Certainly the rapid growth of over 160 reading rooms in the county at one time or another provided the working classes with a unique facility for recreation, education and personal development. It may also have been one of the more successful aspects of the temperance movement. But there was a high failure rate and a steady decline in numbers even in the larger and well provided institutions. By the 1920s changes in the living conditions of the village labourers and in social attitudes had made the reading rooms, as originally planned, less relevant if not obsolete. However, it must be recognised that for a period of about 40 or 50 years in the later 19th and early 20th centuries, the reading room was a major feature of most Wiltshire villages and provided the special facilities which were particularly beneficial to the working classes.

Wiltshire Village Reading Rooms

Brief Gazetteer

WCH Wiltshire Community History website
VCH Victoria County History: Wiltshire
WSA Wiltshire and Swindon Archives
WBR   Wiltshire Buildings Record
O.S. 6in Ordnance Survey 6in map Wiltshire
I.R. Inland Revenue map 1910, WSA L8/1
Kelly Kelly's Directories
Lucy Lucy's Local Directory, Marlborough and District
TNA The National Archives

Aldbourne A reading room, subscription a penny a week, was opened at Wall Cottage in 1892. *WCH*

Alderbury A reading room was opened in 1870 with the support of the Earl of Radnor and Canon Hutchings. Two rooms were rented in the former Old Goose Inn. Some time before 1910 new premises were acquired. A timber building, the gift of Canon Hutchings, consisting of a lobby, two rooms and a separate caretaker's cottage, was erected on a site in Old Road given by the Earl of Radnor. Attendances declined after the Second World War and the Reading Room was closed in 1965. The buildings were demolished in the 1980s. *Kelly 1927, 1939; O.S. 6in 1926; WSA 1966/43, 3476/1/2*

All Cannings *(pl. 1)* The first reading room was recorded as existing in 1872 although it had ceased to exist by 1909. Then in 1914 the village store and post

Alderbury

office was bought by Mary Watney and, in accordance with her will in 1918, was converted to a reading room, a brick and slate building of two rooms. The running costs were mostly met by the rent from the paddock which was part of the charity. It was still being used as a reading room in 1931. In 1971 the room was converted into a village hall. *Kelly 1939; VCH vol 10; WSA L2/50; Salisbury Journal 27 Jan 1872*

Alvediston A reading room is shown on the 1926 Ordnance Survey 6in map. *O.S. 6in 1926*

Ansty A recreation room/hut is recorded in 1927 and again in 1939. *Kelly 1927, 1939*

Ashton Keynes The Working Men's Club and Coffee Room was opened in 1884. It was in rooms rented from Mrs. Wilkins at £13 a year, the cost being met by Capt. Salmon and Capt. Dickenson. There was also a library with a nucleus of 58 books given by Capt Salmon. More books were added later to form a quite substantial library. Women were given some access but were not allowed in the room after 5 p.m. In 1884-5 the average weekly attendance was 76 but this had declined to 25 by 1900-01. In 1905 it was re-opened as the Sports Club but still took 2 daily papers and some weeklies. The building continued in use until about 1914. *Kelly 1890, 1899; WSA 946/112, 113, 115, 116, 123, 124, 125, 136; Madge Paterson and Ernie Ward 'Ashton Keynes: A Village with no history'*

Atworth *(pls. 2, 3)* A Working Men's Institute was established in 1874 through the efforts of Mr. G. Fuller of Neston Park. Subscription was sixpence a month. A new building, given by Mr. G.P.Fuller, was opened by his wife on 16 August 1913 (foundation stone) and contained a reading room, a games room, a room for juniors and three slipper baths which were removed in 1963. The building remains as the village hall. *Kelly 1885, 1890, 1927, 1939; WCH; O.S. 6in 1926; Wiltshire Times 28 Nov 1874, 18 Jan 1879*

Avebury A reading room is recorded as being in existence in 1884. The average weekly attendance was then said to be 78. Musical evenings were an important part of its activities. *Marlborough Times 12 Apr 1884*

Axford   In March 1895 Lady Burdett gave a tea in the reading room for about 50 men and boys. It was then said that the room had been open for 10 years. Sir Francis Burdett was thanked for his generosity in providing lighting and firing. *Marlborough Times 30 Mar 1895, 7 Apr 1900, 13 Jan 1911*

Barford St. Martin A reading room is recorded as being in existence in 1911 and was still running in 1927. It is shown on the 1926 Ordnance Survey map but there is now no trace of it. *Kelly 1911, 1927; O.S. 6in 1926*

Beanacre A reading room on a 'humble scale' was opened in a cottage in January 1882. *Wiltshire Times 28 Jan 1882*

Berwick St. James The AGM of the reading room in 1896 was described as the 4th annual meeting.   The Victoria County History refers to a row of estate cottages and a reading room of c.1900. *VCH vol 15; Wiltshire Times 28 Nov 1896, 15 Jan 1898*

Biddestone A reading room is reported as having been on the Green but at some stage this became a private house. *Kelly 1927, 1939; WCH*

Bishopstone (north)   In 1884 the vicar, Rev. Allan Pile with the churchwardens, purchased from the Ecclesiastical Commissioners for £30 a site of about 15 perches on which was a dilapidated cottage. It was the intention to knock down the cottage and build a reading room but this was never achieved. In 1901 the land was being used as a garden by the schoolmaster paying a rent of 10s a year. *Kelly 1911, 1927, 1939; WSA 1364/12; Charity Commissioners Report 1901-2*

Bishopstone (south) *(pl. 4)* A parish institute was opened in 1885, the gift of Mr. Edwin Dibben. Standing on a site given by Lord Pembroke, it measured 50 ft by 25 ft and was capable of holding 250 people. It was intended to serve several purposes – a mission room, a place for meetings and entertainments, and a reading room with a supply of daily newspapers and games. *Salisbury Journal 21 Feb 1885*

Bishopstrow A reading room had been erected at some stage on a piece of glebe land on the south-west of Church Close adjoining the road leading to Watery Lane. In 1927 it was occupied by Bishopstrow Men's Club who signed a formal tenancy agreement with the vicar. *WSA 1705/4*

Bradenstoke In 1889 Sir Gabriel Gouldney purchased two cottages situated in the village street at Clack and presented these to the village for use as a reading room. After several alterations were made, the room opened in 1890. One room was used for reading and smoking and the other for games. The reading room was still being used in 1927 during the winter months. *Kelly 1899, 1911, 1927; Wiltshire Times 11 Jan 1890*

Bradford-on-Avon In 1879 Rev. Thring built a Temperance Tavern at the bottom of Horse Street on the site of the previous White Hart. This was then leased to the Bradford branch of the Church of England Temperance Society. On the ground floor there was a bar for non-intoxicating beverages and coffee, smoking and bagatelle rooms, a reading room and library. Upstairs there were three bedrooms to be let to artisans and others requiring short-term lodgings. The building was converted after 1900 to become Knees' Household Furnishing store. *Wiltshire Times 9 Aug 1879*

Bradford-on-Avon (A second reading room) In 1863 Rev. G. Melhuish opened a reading room and library solely for men in the vicinity of the parish church. He was said to be indefatigable in his exercises for the intellectual advancement of the poor. *Bristol Mercury 4 Apr 1863*

Bratton   The reading room was mentioned in 1867 as being recently established and in 1882 had between 60 and 70 members. In 1883 a Temperance movement coffee tavern was opened in the buildings of the previous White Horse Inn and the reading room society considered moving there but it is not known whether this actually happened. *Kelly 1939; Wiltshire Times 26 Jan 1867, 23 Sep 1882, 6 Jan 1883, 27 Oct 1883, 9 Apr 1910*

Bremhill *(pl. 5)* The Workman's Institute opened in 1882, the first of five reading rooms established by Lord Fitzmaurice and the Marquess of Lansdowne on the Bowood Estate. An important feature of the Institute was its library. Membership had declined very considerably by 1921 and the possible closure of the room was considered. A new committee was then formed to try to revitalise the institution but this was not successful and the room was closed again in 1924. It is now part of a private house. *Kelly 1885, 1890, 1899, 1911, 1927, 1939; WSA 1154/51; Wiltshire Times 18 Nov 1882*

Brinkworth   A reading room was already in existence in 1920 but it was then decided to replace it. After some long discussion about what type of building should be erected, an ex-army hut from Chiseldon Camp, measuring 60 ft by 20 ft, was purchased and sited on the Malmesbury to Swindon road near the junction to Grittenham. The building no longer exists. There also seems to have been a Working Mens' Club in Church Green, originally built by the G.W.R. for its workers. It closed but was then reopened during the First World War especially for soldiers at home on leave. This building is now part of a private house. *Kelly 1927, 1939; WSA 3509/4/1; Greener and Clothier 'Brinkworth with Grittenham'*

Brixton Deverill   The reading room, probably built in the 19th century, was attached to the Rectory as was the schoolroom. The reading room is now incorporated into the house, The Old Rectory, and serves as the breakfast room. *O.S. 6 in 1926; WSA 662/49*

Broad Chalke In 1908 the Social Committee of King's College, Cambridge (the patron of the church) offered to supply the village with a reading room. A site, on which there had previously been two cottages but then demolished, was provided by Lord Pembroke. The building consisted of a hall which could be divided into two rooms. It was said to have been built from bricks cast by local farmers. It opened in 1911 having cost £280 of which King's College contributed £120.

It became the village hall in 1945. *Kelly 1927; VCH vol 13; Broad Chalke village website; 'Broad Chalke by the People of the Village' 1999*

Broad Hinton In 1881 the vicar opened a coffee tavern but this soon failed. A reading room was said to be 'newly established' in 1884. This could possibly have been in Church House. *Kelly 1890, 1899; VCH vol 12; Marlborough Times 13 Dec 1884; 'Images of a Wiltshire Downland Village: Broad Hinton' 2000*

Bromham *(pl. 6)* The Hope Coffee Tavern and Mission Room was built in 1884 by Miss Julia Edgell, daughter of the vicar, on the site of the old school which had become redundant in 1865. It had two storeys: on the east side of the ground floor was a coffee room and manager's accommodation and a reading room on the west. The reading room also had a library which, in 1899, was reported to have 400 books. On the first floor reached by a separate staircase was the Mission Hall. The building was extended in 1909 with a room 14 ft by 15 ft. This became the reading room with the original reading room becoming the games room. In 1920 the room which had been the coffee tavern was incorporated into the manager's living accommodation. The Mission hall continued to be used by a variety of clubs and organisations until the 1980s but the use declined and the building was in such a poor state of repair by 1988 that it was sold and converted into two cottages.

The Working Men's Club was quite separate and developed out of the original benefit club. *Kelly 1927; WSA 2816/155/5; Wiltshire Times 18 Feb 1882; Devizes Gazette 5 Feb 1891, 12 Jan 1899; Dennis Powney*

Broughton Gifford *(pl. 7)* The building was erected in about 1828 as a Wesleyan chapel. When a new chapel was built in 1907, the old one was bought by Sir Charles Hobhouse and presented to the village to be used as a reading room. It ceased to be a reading room and was sold by auction in 1937 for £40 to Mr. Morris. It was then described as having an entrance hall with a pair of wooden doors leading to a room about 24 ft by 15 ft and a platform at the end. It still had some of the reading room furnishings including tables, chairs and a folding bagatelle board. It is now a private house. *WSA 1865/365; Cobb and Farr sale particulars*

Bulford There is a reference in 1889 to an entertainment of vocal and instrumental music given in the reading room. During the First World War it was used as a

Church of England Soldiers' Institute. It was replaced by a new village hall in the 1980s. *WCH; VCH vol 15; O.S. 6in 1926; Salisbury Journal 2 Feb 1889.*

A special mission room/reading room was set up in 1900 by the Navvy Mission Society for navvies and carpenters building the new huts at Bulford Camp. It used one of the new huts which was said to be capable of holding 400 men. On Sundays there was a bible class and a shortened form of evensong, on one night a week religious teaching, on Thursday entertainments and, on the other nights, a reading and recreation room with plenty of newspapers and games. It was to be used until the camp was completed. *Devizes Gazette 20 Sep 1900*

Burbage There is a reference in 1884 to a concert to raise funds for the reading room which had been established in the village mainly through the effort of the vicar, Rev. Plowman. *O.S. 6in 1926; Marlborough Times 13 Dec 1884*

Burcombe There is a reference to the village reading room in 1927 and again in 1939. *Kelly 1927, 1939*

Calstone Wellington *(pl. 8)* The reading room of stone with red brick dressings was built in 1884 by Lord Fitzmaurice and the Marquess of Lansdowne. It was situated at the road junction south of Sprays Farm. The room was described as lofty with a very cheerful and comfortable appearance. Originally it was open all day from 10 a.m. to 9 p.m. under the management of Mrs. Bowsher. A free lending library was attached. Now it is part of a private house built at the same time as the reading room. *Kelly 1890, 1899, 1911, 1927, 1939; O.S. 6in 1925; VCH vol 17; Wiltshire Times 4 Oct 1884*

Castle Combe There is a reference to a concert in aid of the reading room in 1896. Reading Room Cottage (marked Memorial Cottage on the O.S. map) is situated in The Street. *Wiltshire Times 11 Jan 1896; listed building (1960)*

Castle Eaton A reading room was erected in 1901 by Lt. Col. Archer. It was still recorded as in existence in 1939. *Kelly 1911, 1927, 1939*

Charlcutt A Workmen's Institute including a reading room and library was provided by Lord Fitzmaurice and the Marquess of Lansdowne in 1883. It was situated at Charlecote Hill on the road from Bremhill to Spirthill. It was still in existence as a charity in 1952 but is now a private house/business. *Kelly 1880, 1890, 1899, 1911, 1927, 1939; WSA L2/39; O.S. 6in 1925*

Cherhill   The building, which has been variously called the Reading Room and the Memorial Hall, was erected in 1920 as a First World War memorial. It consisted of two ex-YMCA huts from Yatesbury airfield, bought and presented to the village by the Cooperative Wholesale Society. These were erected next to the school with the front hut (65ft by 21ft) connected by a short corridor to the rear hut (65ft by 16ft) which was mainly used as a skittle alley. In 1927 and again in 1929 authority was obtained to hold domestic science classes for the local schools in the skittle alley. *Kelly 1927, 1939; TNA ED 70/2521; J.H.Blackford 'The Manor and Village of Cherhill'*

Chicklade   A small school was built in 1848 and at a later stage a chapel was added. By 1881 the school had only 11 pupils and by 1892 it had closed. It was then used as a reading room and vestry hall.   *Chicklade website*

Chilmark   *(pl. 9)* A reading room with a library was said to have been lately established in 1894. It was managed by a committee of working men under the presidency of the vicar, Rev. G. Williams, and had 39 members. A new reading and recreation room was erected by Hugh Morrison in 1910. It is now used as the village hall. *Kelly 1911, 1927, 1939; O.S. 6in 1926; Warminster Journal 20 Oct 1894*

Chirton   A concert in aid of the reading room was held in 1906. *Wiltshire Gazette and Herald 3 May 1906*

Chiseldon   *(pls. 10, 11)* A Working Men's Reading Room was opened in 1878 with the support of H. Calley. In 1879, when it was said to have over 50 members, an appeal was made for funds to start a library. By 1882 a coffee tavern had been added and its tariff was being advertised in the local press. The first room was probably in a cottage (now Glebe Cottage) in Church Street. It seems to have been later moved to another cottage (Corner Thatches) in Mays Lane. *Kelly 1885, 1889; Wiltshire and Gloucester Standard 26 Apr 1879, North Wilts Herald Feb 1882; Sheila Passmore*

Chitterne   A small, single storey building called the Penny Reading Room existed in 1891. Now only the gable end remains. It was replaced in 1920-21 by an ex-army hut. *Chitterne website; Sue Robinson 'Chitterne, a Wiltshire Village'*

Chittoe   A series of concerts was held in 1885-6 in aid of the reading room. This was superseded in 1908 by the Workmen's Institute which was established, with the permission of Captain Spicer, in the old schoolroom which had closed in 1906. It was open every evening except Saturday and Sunday but during winter only.   *WSA 2379/36; Wiltshire Times 12 Dec 1885, 16 Jan 1886*

Clevancy   This small hamlet, part of the parish of Hilmarton, consisted of two farms. In 1900 Mr. Sandeman, one of the owners, opened a 'capital' reading room for the free use of all residents in the hamlet. *Devizes Gazette 4 Jan 1900*

Codford St. Mary   *(pl. 12)* A new purpose-built reading room was opened in 1893 being the gift of Alfred Blake of Codford St. Peter. The building was of red brick, pointed black and with Bath stone facings, and the initials A.B. over the entrance. It consisted of one large panelled room 18 ft square and 11 ft high with two fireplaces. It was still in existence in 1911. After it closed, it was at one stage used as a shop and now is a private house. *Kelly 1911; Wiltshire Times 28 Oct 1893, 4 Nov 1893; Warminster Journal 11 Mar 1893, 4 Nov 1893*

Collingbourne Kingston   *(pl. 13)* Immediately after the First World War a reading room was established in an old Y.M.C.A. hut on a site near the railway but this burnt down in 1936. In 1938 Alfred May of Manor Farm gave to the village a piece of land on the road to Brunton containing 22 perches for the establishment of a reading room/village hall in commemoration of the reign of George V. *WSA 2158/14; Collingbourne Kingston website*

Corsham Neston   *(pl. 39)* The Neston Club and Institute was built in 1897 and given to the village by G.P.Fuller of Neston Park. It originally contained a reading room and a games room with a caretaker's house attached. It was extended in 1903 by the addition of a large room at the rear. It continued as a Workmen's Club until 1996 and is now a private house. *Kelly 1927; WSA 3263/13, G3/760/194*

Corsham Pickwick   In 1897 a concert was held to raise funds for the Pickwick Working Men's Institute. *Wiltshire Times 8 Feb 1897*

Corsley   *(pl. 14)* A reading room at Corsley Heath was established in the late 19th century but the accommodation was soon found to be inadequate. In 1892 a new, substantial building was erected on a site 50 yards away given by Lord

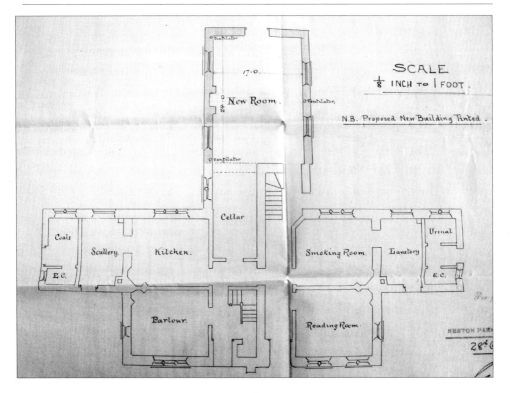

Neston (Corsham) Plan

Bath. The building cost £300 and was partly funded by a loan from Mr. Cookson of Sturford Mead.   It was very active in the 1890s but declined after 1900 with only thirty members in 1905. The building was extended in 1925 and is still in use. *Kelly 1899, 1911, 1927, 1939; WCH; O.S. 6in 1926; Wiltshire Times 13 Jan 1894; Warminster Journal 15 Oct 1892, 29 Oct 1892,1 Apr 1893, 16 Dec 1893, 3 Feb 1894, 17 Feb 1894, 24 Feb 1894, 15 Dec 1894, 16 Feb 1895, 16 Mar 1895; M.F.Davies 'Life in an English Village: Corsley' 1909*

Corston   *(pl. 15)* The reading room building on the main road through the village celebrated its centenary in 2004. It is now used as the village hall. *O.S. 6in 1925; Swindon Advertiser 8 Apr 2004*

Crockerton (see Longbridge Deverill)

Crudwell A reading room is mentioned in 1885 and 1889. *Kelly 1885, 1889*

Dauntsey Green The Meux estate sale in 1906 included a reading room adjoining

1 All Cannings

2 Atworth: Working Men's Institute (1874)

3 Atworth: Reading Room (1913)

4 Bishopstone (south)

5 Bremhill

6 Bromham

7 Broughton Gifford

8 Calstone Wellington

9 Chilmark

10 Chiseldon, Glebe Cottage (© Sheila Passmore)

11 Chiseldon, May's Lane (© Sheila Passmore)

12 Codford (© Sally Thomson)

13 Collingbourne Kingston

14 Corsley

15 Corston

16 Derry Hill

17 East Grimstead

18 East Knoyle

THE BUILDING NEWS, MAY 16. 1884.

A Village Dispensary and Parish Room
built at East Kennett Marlborough

For the Exors. of the late Miss Mathews.

C.E. PONTING ARCHT.
MARLBOROUGH.

19 East Kennett (The Builder); see p. 92 for enlargement of plan.

20 East Kennett

21 Easton Royal

22 Enford

23 Fonthill Gifford

24 Foxham

25 Farley

26 Fonthill Bishop

27 Great Bedwyn

28 Great Somerford

29 Hanging Langford

30 Hannington

31 Heytesbury

32 Hindon

33 Holt

34 Malmesbury

35 Manningford Bruce

36 Manton

37 Marden

38 Market Lavington

39 Neston (Corsham)

40 Netheravon

41 Newton Tony (© Chris Talbot)

42 Nomansland

43 Market Lavington

44 Purton

45 Potterne

46 Purton

47 Purton Stoke (© English Heritage National Monuments Record)

48 Redlynch

49 Rowde (© Rowde Village Website)

50 South Wraxall

51 Stratford-sub-Castle (© Trish Steel)

52 Teffont Evias

53 Teffont Magna

54 Tisbury

55 Turleigh

56 Upavon

57 Whitley

58 Worton

Dauntsey

a cottage (Post Office). A reading room is shown on the 1926 Ordnance Survey 6in map. *O.S. 6in 1925; WSA 106/3, 3476/1/109*

Derry Hill *(pl. 16)* The Working Men's Club and Institute was opened in 1873 in the premises of the old National School with the support of Lord Fitzmaurice. In 1875 it had 110 members and a library containing 790 volumes. A Fife and Drum Band was re-started in 1882. At some later stage it became the village hall but is now a private house. *Kelly 1880, 1890, 1911, 1939; VCH vol 17; Wiltshire Independent 11 Feb 1875, 9 Mar 1876; Wiltshire Times 3 Feb 1883, 16 May 1885, 23 Jan 1886, 8 Jan 1910; Devizes Gazette 21 Oct 1897*

Dilton Marsh A reading room was opened in 1880 in a converted building opposite the church. It contained two rooms; one was 15 ft square and the other 12 ft square. Around the room were mottoes arranged by the Misses Phipps (e.g. 'Keep good men company and you shall be one of the number' and 'Good words quench more than a bucket of water'). The rent was paid for the first five years by Mr. C. Phipps, the president. *Wiltshire Times 17 Jan 1880*

Donhead St. Andrew A reading room was mentioned in 1927. It is now a private house. *Kelly 1927; Humbert sale particulars*

Donhead St. Mary Two former schools stand to the north-west of the church. One of brick, stone and thatch was once used as a reading room. *VCH vol 13*

Downton A Reading Room and Institute was mentioned in 1875. *Kelly 1880, 1885, 1899; Salisbury Journal 16 Jan 1875, 19 Feb 1881*

Durrington In 1912 a group of villagers bought the old school house to establish a reading and recreation room. In 1924 it was considered too small and was sold to the parochial church council, the proceeds being used towards the cost of a new hall. The old room continued to be used for smaller groups. *WSA D375/2/12*

Easterton A reading room, the gift of Charles Hitchcock, is mentioned in 1885. *Kelly 1885, 1890*

East Grimstead *(pl. 17)* The present reading room (village hall) was built in 1995. It replaced a corrugated iron building which was opened in December 1922. *Richard Peacham*

East Kennett *(pls. 19, 20; and p.92)* In 1883 a bequest by Miss Matthews was used to erect a substantial building, designed by C. Ponting of Marlborough and built by S.Elliott of Newbury at a cost of £1029, containing a dispensary, a reading room and living accommodation. The lofty reading room measured 43ft by 17 ft. The foundation stone was laid by Miss E. Fisher, niece of Miss Matthews, in June 1883 and the building was said to have been opened in November 1883. By 1891 it was well supported by honorary members and others paying 1d. a week. It had a nucleus of a library, a bagatelle board and several sets of draughts and dominoes. The *Graphic, Fun,* the *Standard* and the local papers were always available. The reading room was open from 6 p.m. to 9 p.m. during the winter months. Now East Kennett House. *Marlborough Times 28 Apr 1883, 9 Jun 1883; Lucy 1891; O.S. 6in 1925; The Building News 16 May 1884; VCH vol 12; Kennet conservation website; David Snape*

East Knoyle *(pl. 18)* **A** reading room was in existence by 1889 when it was particularly frequented by the visiting workmen who were rebuilding Clouds. It then met in either the National School or the Chapel schoolroom. In 1908 a new hall/reading room was built and presented to the village by Isabella, widow of Alfred Seymour of Knoyle House. It incorporated part of an earlier 14th century building, the east wing becoming the billiard room. It had an original membership of 40. A library was started with a gift of over 30 books and a bookcase by Mr. Norton who was staying at Knoyle House. *Kelly 1927; Salisbury Journal 2 Nov 1889; Anthony Claydon*

Easton Royal *(pl. 21)* A reading room was established in the village in 1895 on the initiative of Mr. J. Haines. When it closed for the summer months, a cricket club was established to take its place with Rev. Kemm as captain. It was allowed to use the Wind Mill meadow. A cottage called Library Cottage is said to be the old reading room. *Marlborough Times 19 Jan 1895, 27 Apr 1895; O.S. 6in 1926; Kennet conservation site*

Edington A reading room was in existence in 1909 but it probably closed soon after this. *WSA 2222/32*

Enford *(pl. 22)* A reading room was established around 1885, using the school room. In the early 20th century a wooden hut was erected for the reading room and this remains as the village hall. *Wiltshire Telegraph 10 Jan 1885; O.S. 6in 1925; Kennet conservation website*

Erlestoke A reading room was in existence around 1900. It opened on four nights a week in winter – Monday, Wednesday, Friday and Saturday. Subscriptions were 6d a month or 2d a week. It seems to have been held in the school for rule no. 7 stipulated 'Member to put out lights at closing time and leave room ready for school the next day.' *WSA 1724/13*

Farley *(pl. 23)* A reading room seems to have been in existence by 1879. At one stage it was held in a cottage, part of the Almshouses. This proved inconvenient for the almshouse inhabitants and the room was closed. In 1902 the vicar, Rev. Henderson, successfully led a campaign to build a new reading room/village hall in the school playground. Part of the funding came from the surplus school funds after the County Education Committee took over responsibility for elementary schools and there was a generous subscription from Earl Radnor. The new building was of corrugated iron and remains in use as the village hall. *Salisbury Journal 19 Oct 1889; Miss Henderson 'History of the Farley Reading Room' 1936 (unpublished)*

Figheldean A parish library was established by the vicar, Henry Carswell, in the mid-19th century and by 1864 had 70 to 80 members. This seems to have been incorporated in a reading room erected in 1891, the gift of George Knowles. *Kelly 1899, 1911; VCH vol 15*

Fonthill Bishop *(pl. 24)* The reading room was erected by the Morrison family and remains part of the Fonthill estate. The stone building has the inscription HM 1912 on the gable end. In the 1930s it developed into a men's club which, apart from the usual newspapers and games, was noted for its annual outings. In 1935 electric lights replaced the old oil lamps. *Fonthill estate archives, 1271*

Fonthill Gifford *(pl. 23)* An early reading room, which had been closed by 1928, was then re-opened but only lasted until 1935. In 1939 the trustees obtained from Mary Stewart of Fonthill Abbey a lease for 14 years of a piece of land on the north side of Stop Street 'on which stands the village hall to be used as a recreation and reading room'. It remains as a wooden building with a galvanised iron roof. *WSA 1855/37; O.S. 6in 1926; Fonthill estate archives 2287*

Fovant In 1885 a church hall (an iron building 40 ft by 20 ft) was erected by Rev. Earle on a site given by the Earl of Pembroke. It was also used by working men for reading and recreation. It was destroyed by fire in 1908 and a new hall erected in its place. In 1970 the Parish Council purchased the building and renamed it the Village Hall. Now demolished. *Kelly 1890, 1911, 1927; O.S. 6in 1926; Salisbury Journal 6 Nov 1886; Fovant website*

Foxham *(pl. 24)* A small library had been established in the 19th century and this was moved in 1884 to a new reading room erected by Lord Fitzmaurice and the Marquess of Lansdowne. This was a substantial stone building, 28 ft by 18 ft, together with a caretaker's house. It was still in existence in 1939 but by the 1960s it was just a charitable trust with income from the use of the hall and rent from the caretaker's cottage. It is still in community use. *Kelly 1880, 1885, 1899, 1911, 1927, 1939; Wiltshire Times 27 Sep 1884; WSA 1154/59; WBR*

Goatacre A reading room is mentioned in 1890. *Kelly 1890*

Great Bedwyn *(pl. 27)* The building in Church Street is still called The Old Reading Room (now a hairdresser's).   In 1913 authority was given for domestic science lessons to be held there for pupils from Great Bedwyn and Little Bedwyn schools. It was then still in the ownership of the Marquess of Ailesbury. *TNA ED70/2539*

Great Somerford *(pl. 28)* A reading room was erected by Walter Powell in 1872. This was a red brick structure with arched windows, a high gabled roof and a small ornate porch. A caretaker's house in similar style was attached at one side. When Powell died in 1882, all his property was sold at auction and the reading room became a Primitive Methodist chapel. *Kelly 1890, 1927; WSA 212A/38/34/10; Portia Hobbs 'Walter Powell'*

Grittleton A reading and recreation room was erected by subscription in 1902 as a memorial to Rev. Henry Boldero, rector of the parish 1864-1900. It was a quite ornate building with a reading room measuring 28 ft by 12 ft (with a folding partition) and attached caretaker's house. A surprising feature of the plan is the room marked 'Nurses room'. It is now a private house. *Kelly 1911, 1927, 1939; O.S. 6in 1923; WSA G3/760/126*

Hanging Langford *(pl. 29)* A parish reading room was built in 1913 with extensive improvements in 1928. Later it became the village hall. *WSA 502/47; VCH vol 15*

Hannington *(pl. 30)* A reading room existed by 1899 but the building known as the Old Reading Room (now a private house) has a date stone 1921. *Kelly 1899, 1911, 1939; Hannington conservation site*

Heddington A workman's club was erected in 1881 at a cost of £600. It had a reading room, coffee bar, fives court and quoit ground. The building was later used as a post office. *Kelly 1885, 1890, 1911; O.S. 6in 1926; VCH vol 17*

Heytesbury *(pl. 31)* A reading room was in existence by 1883. This seems to have consisted of a single room although a second room was made available in 1889. In 1894, through the generosity of Lord Heytesbury, they acquired a shop formerly occupied by Mr. Davies. After considerable alteration, it contained a large panelled room for games (including billiards and bagatelle), a smaller reading room and a coffee tavern. There was also accommodation for the caretaker. At some later stage the room seems to have been moved to the old school behind the church. This belonged to Lord Heytesbury but the reading room was allowed to use it rent free. When the Heytesbury estate was sold in

1923 the reading room trustees bought the building (lot 104). It then consisted of a large recreation room and a committee room on the ground floor with caretaker's accommodation above. In 1930 there was a somewhat acrimonious dispute with a neighbouring landowner about right of access. *Kelly 1899, 1911, 1927, 1939; Wiltshire Times 6 Jan 1883, 15 Nov 1884, 24 Oct 1885, 6 Feb 1892, 4 Nov 1883, 13 Jan 1894; Warminster Journal 17 Jan 1885, 7 Nov 1885, 8 Sep 1894, 10 Nov 1894, 2 Nov 1895; Salisbury Journal 16 Nov 1889; WSA 859/44, 2132/90; I.R.*

Heywood A reading room seems to have been erected in the later 19th century by Mr. James Burgess. When he died in 1898, his son, Nelson Burgess, sold to Baron Ludlow two cottages and land in Heywood 'together with the reading room and buildings erected by the said James Burgess on the said land .. which reading room is now unoccupied.' *Wiltshire Times 1 Feb 1896; WSA 2270/23*

Highworth A substantial Working Men's Club and Reading Room was in existence by 1878. It also contained a library of over 150 books. In 1879 it was reported to have 118 members and a year later 105 members of whom half were working men. By 1884 it had an annual income of over £300. *Wiltshire and Gloucester Standard 26 Jan 1878, 1 Feb 1879; North Wilts Herald 2 Feb 1880; Swindon Advertiser 16 Feb 1884*

Hilmarton (see also **Clevancy**) A reading room may have existed in 1881 but a purpose-built room was erected in 1892 next to the school by the lord of the manor. It also had a library. In the late 1890s, despite a membership of about 50, the club was running with an annual deficit which was paid off by Sir John Poynder, M.P. In 1899, however, he wrote to say that the time had arrived when the reading room should be self-supporting. This required the establishment of a new committee and arrangements for the room. At the first annual meeting after this, in February 1900, the new scheme was declared a success with sufficient local funds being raised to meet all expenses with a small balance. *Kelly 1899, 1890, 1911, 1927, 1939; Devizes Gazette 12 Feb 1881, 14 Jan 1897, 11 Feb 1897, 3 Feb 1898, 12 Jan 1899, 8 Feb 1900; Wiltshire Times 11 Jan 1896; I.R.*

Hindon *(pl. 32)* A meeting was held in 1883 to consider establishing a reading room. About 80 villagers promised to become members. The reading room was probably in the building known as the Court House which was given to the village by Hugh Morrison in 1922. *Wiltshire Times 10 Nov 1883; Hindon village plan*

Holt   *(pl. 33)* A substantial stone reading room was erected in 1873 on a site presented by T. Forster. Although starting well, interest in the reading room declined and it was closed in summer 1880. There must have been sufficient support to try again for the winter but the room was finally closed in February 1881. At some stage after that, it was used as a wool store. In 1885 a meeting was called with the support of Mr. MacKay, Rev. Mosely and Mr. F. Beaven and there was general agreement to re-open the rooms. The balance in hand of £24 was used to repair the building and a further £12 was spent on furniture. A substantial billiard room measuring 28ft by 18ft was added in 1893. The institute then began to flourish and in 1896 had 100 members. It is now the Holt Institute. A coffee tavern was also opened in the main street by Miss Chapman in 1885. *Kelly 1885, 1890, 1899, 1911, 1927, 1939; O.S. 6in 1926; Wiltshire Times 31 Oct 1874, 20 May 1875, 10 Jul 1880, 17 Oct 1885, 25 Jan 1890, 6 Dec 1890, 13 May 1893, 27 May 1893, 27 Jan 1894, 14 Apr 1894, 1 Dec 1894, 18 Jan 1896, 22 Jan 1898; O.S. 6in 1922; Holt website; WSA 3985/1/1-9; WSA 3985/1/2/1*

Honeystreet   A workmen's hall was in existence in 1880. *Kelly 1880; Lucy 1883, Marlborough Times 26 Jan 1884*

Horningsham   A reading room in a cottage in Church Street was opened in the 1890s. The new village hall erected by Lord Bath in 1930 included a reading room over the billiard room. *Kelly 1899, 1911; Wiltshire Times 7 May 1892; Warminster Journal 10 Mar 1894; WCH; WBR*

Keevil   An iron building capable of holding 300 people was erected in 1892 by Col. Wallington and used for concerts, entertainment, etc. It is not certain whether this also housed a reading room. *Kelly 1927; O.S. 6in 1926; Wiltshire Times 23 Apr 1892*

Lacock   The original reading room was opened in 1854 on Bowden Hill. It had strong support from the vicar, Rev. Blomfield, and from the local gentry including Capt. Gladstone and Henry Talbot. Unusually it was open all day from 9 a.m. to 9.30 p.m. except Sundays. A substantial library was developed quite early on with some 30 books added in 1855 at a cost of £6 9s. It was still in operation in 1939 but later became the parish room and was demolished in the early 1980s. In 1907 General Palmer built, in memory of his son, a Working Men's Institute which contained reading, billiards and other rooms. *Kelly 1911, 1927, 1939; O.S. 6in 1925; Swindon Advertiser 26 Jul 2001; WSA 2198/16; Brian Banks 'Snippets of Lacock Schooling and the Establishment of a Reading Room' WRS Recorder Feb 2008*

Latton A men's club room, the gift of the Earl of St. Germans, was opened in 1910. There is also reference to another building given by the Cooperative Wholesale Society in 1922. *Kelly 1911, 1927, 1939*

Laverstock A reading room was opened in the old schoolroom in 1894. At first it was open every evening except Sunday from 7 p.m. Support waned after 1900 and in 1903 the opening times were reduced to three nights a week, Monday, Wednesday and Friday. It seems to have closed finally in 1916. *WCH; WSA 1324/23*

Limpley Stoke A reading room is mentioned in 1911. It may have been run by or in the property of F.Millard. *Kelly 1911, 1927, 1939; Lewis and Mattingly 'Limpley Stoke'*

Little Cheverell In 1919 a planning application for a reading room was approved. This was a timber or corrugated iron hut with a single room measuring 25ft by 15ft. *WSA G5/760/91*

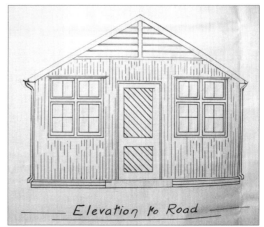

Little Cheverell

Little Somerford A wood and iron building, presented to the village by Walter Powell and built on a site at the foot of Clay Street provided by Mr. Wightwick lord of the manor, was officially opened by Powell in June 1879. In 1890 it was stated to have been closed for a long time through lack of interest and was then sold at auction. *Kelly 1885, 1890; Wiltshire Times 8 Nov 1890; Devizes Gazette 12 Jun 1879; Portia Hobbs 'Walter Powell'*

Longbridge Deverill with Crockerton   In 1893 a reading room of corrugated iron was built on a site given by Lord Bath at Foxholes. This site was deliberately chosen to be convenient for both Longbridge Deverill and Crockerton.   The building cost £100 to erect and furnish and £86 of this was raised by subscriptions including £25 from the Marquess of Bath and £10 each from the vicar and Rev. Morrice, a former vicar of the parish. It opened on only three nights a week with a subscription of 6d a month. *Kelly 1899, 1911, 1927, 1939; O.S. 6in 1926; Warminster Journal 7 Jan 1893, 10 Feb 1894, 7 Apr 1894; Wiltshire Times 7 Apr 1894, 20 Apr 1895*

Lydiard Millicent

Lydiard Millicent   A reading room of corrugated iron was erected by J.H.Sadler of Lydiard House between 1899 and 1910. It stood near the Sun on the south-west side of the Street. In 1922 authority was given to hold domestic science lessons there for local schools. In 1924 it was given to the parish council but sold in 1965 when a new village hall was built. *O.S. 6in 1925; VCH ; WSA 3476/1/210; TNA ED/70/2550; I.R.*

Maiden Bradley A reading room was in existence in 1894 when the members played a draughts and bagatelle match against Horningsham reading room at Maiden Bradley. In the 1920s a reading room club was held in a cottage in the High Street. *Kelly 1939; WCH; Warminster Journal 10 Mar 1894*

Malmesbury *(pl. 34)* A substantial building was erected in 1870 in Silver Street by Walter Powell. It had a frontage of 24 ft on Silver Street and ran a length of 170 ft to the back of the premises. It contained the reading room, a library and accommodation for the caretaker. A notable feature was that it had one room for the upper classes and tradesmen and an inner room for the lower classes. The rooms were decorated with a collection of buck and other horns. The premises were sold in 1882 on the death of Walter Powell but re-purchased the following year by Col Miles, M.P. and then reopened as a reading room. The sale particulars describe a lofty and well-ventilated building with gas and water laid on, a coal cellar and, at the rear, a sitting room, kitchen with cooking range and offices.

There was a light and airy bedroom above with a water closet on the landing. The sale also included 600 books from Powell's various reading rooms. Later the building was used for a technical school and for the town's council chamber. It is now the King's nursery. *Kelly 1885; WSA 212A/38/24/10; Wiltshire and Gloucester Standard 4 Jan 1879; Wiltshire Times 19 Feb 1881, 20 Jan 1883; Portia Hobbs 'Walter Powell'; Charles Vernon 'An Historical Guide to Malmesbury (2005)*

Manningford *(pl. 35)* A reading room is marked on the 1926 O.S. 6in map north of Manningford Bruce. In August 2010 the corrugated iron building, much dilapidated, was about to be demolished. *O.S. 6in 1926; North Wilts Church Magazine Oct 1907*

Manton *(pl. 36)* A reading room on a small scale for working men had existed for some time before 1890, having been started mainly through Mr. Hulme, art master at Marlborough College. It was then decided the village needed larger premises which would serve several purposes – night school, meetings, clubs. The Marquess of Ailesbury made a site available for a small rent in the centre of the village and a new building was erected (the Manton Rooms) at a cost of £250. It contained a large classroom, a reading room and a smoking room. Apart from the reading room, it was used by a variety of village organisations including temperance meetings and sewing classes. The rooms were open every evening throughout the year. In 1931 a village hall was built on the eastern end of the reading room. In 1968 it was sold and became a private house. *Marlborough Times 1 Feb 1890, 15 Feb 1890; Kennet conservation site; Miss Cobern*

Marden *(pl. 37)* The present wooden village hall was originally erected as a reading room in 1923. *Kennet conservation site*

Market Lavington *(pl. 38, 43)* In 1865 a substantial building of brick with giant pilasters, stone details and a rich portico, called the Workman's Hall was erected with funds left by Edward Saunders. The building contained a reading room, coffee bar, kitchen and living rooms for the caretaker on the ground floor and a large lecture hall on the first floor. Edward Saunders had left £500 to build the hall plus another £500 for the temperance association. However, the trustees decided to spend the whole £1000 on building the hall. The total cost, including furnishing, was £1381. It was always very closely linked to the temperance movement, Edward Saunders having stipulated that the strictest temperance rules be adhered to. *Kelly 1885, 1890, 1911, 1927, 1939; WCH; Wiltshire Independent 16 Feb 1865, 10 Feb 1876; Wiltshire Telegraph 17 Jan 1885; Wiltshire Times 11 Apr 1885, 13 Feb 1886, 22 Jan 1910; Charity Commissioners Report 1902-3*

Marston Meysey There is a reference to a reading and coffee room in 1885. *Kelly 1885*

Mere A meeting was held in 1883 to discuss the establishment of a reading room and, as a temporary measure, a cottage next to the Talbot was rented from Mrs. Rumsey. The next year part of the Angel Hotel was purchased and converted to a Church Institute containing a reading room, games room, caretaker's accommodation and a smaller committee room. Ladies were admitted as members but could only use the room from 2 to 5 each afternoon. A library was started in 1885 with a variety of books, mostly secondhand, being bought from Brown and Co., Salisbury. The reading room got into financial difficulties in the 1890s and the accommodation seems to have been given up in 1895 when the contents of the room were sold and the money so raised given to the Church Restoration Fund. *Kelly 1880, 1885, 1890; WSA 2944/88, 2944/126*

Milton Lilbourne A reading room was established in 1894 through the efforts of Mr. F. Ravenhill who collected sufficient subscriptions to cover the cost. The room was open to all men and boys over 14 on payment of a nominal subscription. A committee was formed with the vicar as President. *Marlborough Times 10 Nov 1894*

Monkton Farleigh In 1964 there was a planning application to convert the disused reading room to a private dwelling. This then seems to have been changed to demolishing the reading room and building a bungalow on the land behind it. The site was north west of the church next to the then Post Office. *WSA G2/770/267*

Netheravon *(pl. 40)* The reading room marked on the 1925 O.S. map still exists and is now a library. There is also a reference to a Workmen's Institute opened in 1921 in Old Post Office Lane. *Lucy 1921; O.S. 6in 1925*

Newton Tony *(pl. 41)* The reading room was built next to the churchyard by the rector in the 1860s. The one storey building was converted into a private house c.1915. *VCH vol 15; W.H. Swift 'A Wiltshire Village in the 1860s'.*

Nomansland   *(pl. 42)* A village hall with a reading room was built in North Lane in 1910. It is of brick, covered in roughcast, under a tiled roof and has a verandah and porch on the west side. It consisted of two rooms divided by a movable partition. *Kelly 1927, 1939; VCH vol 11; David Kerridge 'Nomansland – its Two Hundred Years of History' (2002)*

North Bradley   A reading room had been established by 1893 when 40 members attended the annual supper. It was still in existence in 1910 with 50 members attending a supper followed by a smoking concert. *Kelly 1899, 1911; Wiltshire Times 18 Feb 1893, 10 Feb 1894, 1 Feb 1896, 26 Feb 1910*

North Newnton   There is a reference in 1910 to 20 members from the North Newnton reading room going to Market Lavington to play a series of friendly games. *Marlborough Times 25 Feb 1910*

Norton Bavant   In the winter of 1894 the parish room was used as a reading room but this was found to be inconvenient. In 1895 an old carpenter's shop was purchased and converted into a reading room at a cost of £15. It was open daily from 6 to 10 p.m. and initially had 21 members. The main supporters were Mrs. Torrance (Norton House), Mr. Hiscock (a farmer) and the Benett-Stanfords (Pyt House). *Warminster Journal 5 Jan 1895*

Nunton   The Radnor Hall reading room was built in 1893 at the expense of the Earl of Radnor. By 1939 it was used for concerts, dances and meetings. *Kelly 1899, 1911, 1927, 1939*

Oare   The reading room was originally in a rented room in a cottage. When this became no longer available in 1893, Francis Rogers of Rainscombe erected a galvanised building for use as a reading and recreation room. It contained one large and one small room. He transferred ownership to the parish council in 1899. Membership was open to all males over 15 living in Oare and its neighbourhood with a quarterly subscription of 1s. There was also a small lending library called the Ernle library. In 1899 it had 25 members. The room was renovated in 1910 partly with a legacy from Rev. Rogers. The inside was painted green and the ceiling whitened. The outside was also painted and a new coal shed and W.C. added. *Kelly 1911, 1927, 1939; Lucy 1906; WSA 2387/23; Charity Commissioners report 1901; Marlborough Times 7 Oct 1910, 18 Nov 1910*

Ogbourne St. George In 1882 it is reported that the vicar and churchwardens bought a building (possibly an old chapel) for use as a reading room. There is also a reference to the Church Room being erected in 1905 and used as a reading room. *Kelly 1911; VCH vol 12*

Overton A reading room near the church was provided by Lady Meux in 1890. It was said in 1891 to be well lighted and well warmed with comfortable furniture and a nicely stocked library. *Lucy 1891*

Oxenwood A reading room is marked on the 1926 O.S. 6in map. *O.S. 6in 1926*

Pewsey A reading room was in existence in 1884 when the annual meeting was held in the coffee tavern with the vicar presiding. It then had about 20 members. It was still active in 1910 when a games tournament was being held with neighbouring reading rooms. *Kelly 1899, 1903; Marlborough Times 2 Feb 1884; Wiltshire Telegraph 10 Jan 1885; Wilshire Times 15 Oct 1910*

Porton A reading room was opened in 1907 largely thorough the efforts of Mr. Gay (a farmer), who was said to have built the room, and the vicar, Rev. Youngman. It was open to all males over 14 living in the parish of Idmiston including Porton and Gomeldon. In 1912 a rifle club was formed which helped to sustain the reading room financially. The room was closed temporarily in 1915 but seems to have been reopened in 1919. *WCH; WSA 1806/33*

Potterne *(pl. 45)* A Working Men's Social Club and Institute was opened in 1875 at the instigation of the vicar, Archdeacon Buchanan, and the squire, Mr. W. Stancomb. It was originally held in a cottage near Mr. Stancomb's entrance lodge and had a membership of 45. A new building was erected next to the school in 1908. *Kelly 1890, 1911, 1927; Wiltshire Independent 13 Jan 1876, 27 Jan 1876; Wiltshire Times 20 Jan 1883; WSA 1172/66*

A separate Parochial Temperance Club was opened in 1899 by the Parochial Temperance Association. It had premises adjoining the King's Arms and its three rooms were equipped with a variety of games, including a bagatelle table and an 'adapted' billiard table, plus newspapers and books. It was said that there was plenty of room in the village for this club as well as the Working Men's Institute. *Devizes Gazette 14 Dec 1899*

Purton *(pl.44, 46)* The Workmen's Institute was built in 1879 on the site of the old charity school by James Sadler of Lydiard Millicent in memory of Mrs. Sadler's sister at a cost of £3000. Previously the school room had been used as a parish reading room. The new building consisted of a reading room, a large public room capable of seating 300, a tea and coffee room, a smoking room and accommodation for the caretaker. It was officially opened in 1880 by the Earl of Shaftesbury. Despite the very good facilities it does not seem to have been a great success and was always in debt. The Charity Commission report of 1902 says that the building is now let by the Parish Council to Henry Borton. It is now the library with a museum on the first floor. *Kelly 1885 ,1899, 1927, 1939; O.S. 6in 1925; North Wilts Herald 5 Jan 1880; Charity Commissioners Report 1902; Alec Robbins 'Purton's Past'*

Purton Stoke *(pl. 47)* An iron building was erected in 1908 largely by the effort of Miss Warrender of Purton Stoke House. It was used as a Christian Reading Room and as a meeting place/hall. Some time after 1972 it was bought by the Young Farmers Club and is now used as their meeting place. *Kelly 1939; O.S. 6in 1925; Purton Stoke website*

Ramsbury A reading room was first established soon after 1858 by Mr. Batson but, after a short time, he converted this to a Night School. A new reading room was erected in 1883 (next to the present fire station) by Mr. Batson with the support of Lady Burdett. In 1894 it had 37 members and was still being heavily subsidised by Lady Burdett. A soup kitchen was also set up there where the poor could get a bowl of soup for 1d. *Marlborough Times 29 Mar 1890; WSA 2872/425, 2872/427; Barbara Croucher 'Ramsbury: The Village in the Valley'*

Redlynch *(pl. 48)* The reading room or workmen's hall was erected between 1875 and 1880 by William Taunton, a local farmer. In 1889 additional rooms were added, with an entrance in Petticoat Lane, in his memory by his widow and children. It is now a private house. *Kelly 1880, 1885, 1899, 1911; WCH; VCH vol 11, Jenny Bowman/Peter Daniels*

Roundway A reading room of timber and corrugated iron was erected by Edward Coward probably around 1900. Leases were granted in 1938 and 1967 by the Commissioner of Crown Lands to the Southbroom Parochial Church Council. *WCH; WSA 594/52*

Rowde *(pl. 49)* A reading and coffee room was erected in 1887 by Mrs. Starkey in memory of her son, Andrew, who had been vicar of Rowde from 1864 to 1871 but who had died at the age of 33. Attached was a cottage for the caretaker. The building was enlarged in 1896 by C.H.Lowe and then also contained a library. The building is now the village hall. *Kelly 1890, 1899, 1911, 1939; Devizes Gazette 28 Jan 1897; Charity Commissioners Report 1902; Rowde village hall website*

Salisbury St. Martin's A committee of 5 gentlemen and 10 working men was set up in 1876 under the chairmanship of Rev. S. Mangin to establish a working men's club in the parish. A public appeal was made for donations to meet the cost of about £70. Mr. Ryder the M.P. gave five guineas. The club was opened in September in rooms in St. Ann St. and started with 177 members. *Salisbury Journal 4 Dec 1875, 27 Apr 1876, 23 Sep 1876, 30 Sep 1876*

Seend Wadham Locke built a reading room in Pelch Lane for the employees of the iron works but the use of this hall was given to the school in 1877. A Workmen's Reading Room was opened in 1881 in rented premises in The Street and this became the Workmen's Club in 1884. It closed in 1894 but was revived in 1902. The Club was provided by Mrs. Russell in 1922 with an ex-army hut in Rusty Lane. This was replaced by the present village hall in the 1970s. *O.S. 6in 1926; WCH; Seend Community website; Edward Bradby 'Seend'*

Semley A reading room is recorded as being in existence in 1927 and may be the building labelled 'Institute' on the 1926 Ordnance Survey map. *Kelly 1927, 1939; O.S.6in 1926*

Shaw and Whitley *(pl. 57)* The first reading room was opened in 1884 being built and furnished by Mr. Fuller. It was open every weekday from noon till 9.30 p.m. and very quickly had 50 members. In 1890 it was made free, the cost being met by Mr. Fuller and Mr. Shadwell of Meadowbank. In January 1897 it was reported that the room had been closed for three years and was being converted into a shop. Mr. Wiltshere then offered the use of a large room at the back of the house and the reading room was re-opened there. This soon proved to be too small but a completely new building was not erected until 1904. This building bears a foundation stone by Mr. J. Stancomb. It now acts as the Whitley village hall having been extended in 1966. *Kelly 1927, 1939; Wiltshire Times 5 Jan 1884, 11 Jan 1890, 29 Nov 1890, 16 May 1891, 24 Oct 1891, 14 Jan 1893; WSA G2/770/312*

Sherston There is a reference to a reading room being in existence in 1895. *Kelly 1895*

Shrewton In December 1900 a reading room was said to have been recently opened. It had 60 members. Subscriptions were 5s. a year or 6d a month with an entrance fee of 6d. *Devizes Gazette 22 Dec 1900*

South Wraxall   *(pl. 50)* A church institute and reading room was erected by subscription in 1903. It is a corrugated iron building which was still in use in 1927 and still exists today. *Kelly 1911, 1927, 1939; O.S. 6in 1926*

Southwick There is a reference to a reading room being in existence in 1895. *Kelly 1895*

Stanton St. Quintin A reading room was opened in Lower Stanton in 1920. It reopened in 1953 after a break but was later demolished. *WCH; WSA 1621/37*

Staverton   In 1919 a reading room was opened by public subscription in a hut purchased from the Red Cross hospital in Trowbridge. The total cost of the hut and its furnishing was £100, £63 of which was raised by a village collection together with a donation from Nestle which had a factory in the village. A second hut was acquired the next year and equipped with a billiard table and a library. *O.S. 6in 1922; WSA G2/770/474; Pete Lavis 'The Book of Staverton' (2002)*

Steeple Ashton   In 1886 a club and institute was opened in a house provided by Mr. Long M.P. A library was also established, the nucleus of which came from books donated by the Rebecca Hussey charity (London). At a later stage it was replaced by a corrugated iron building. *Wiltshire Times 16 Oct 1886, 7 Aug 2009; WSA 730/328*

Steeple Langford A private room in the village was used as a parish reading room until 1909. *Kelly 1899; VCH vol 15*

Stourton There is a reference to the Stourton Club and Reading Room in 1927.
Kelly 1927

Stratton St Margaret

Stratton St. Margaret In the 1890s a reading room was established in an old
railway carriage in the vicarage garden. Two iron buildings, one as a billiard
room, were added later. At some time the railway carriage was replaced by a brick
building. *Frederick Fuller 'Stratton in Camera'*

Stratford-sub-Castle   *(pl. 51)* A reading room was built in about 1881 mainly
through the efforts of Mrs. Mary King, wife of Canon King, vicar from 1849 to
1884. It also had a lending library. The room was open to all male parishioners
over 16 during the winter months on every evening from 6.30 to 9 p.m. except
Saturday and Sunday. In 1886 it had 29 members but this declined to only 9
ordinary and 12 honorary members in 1892. An attempt was made by the vicar
in 1905 to increase membership and to make the reading room financially viable.
It now serves as the village hall. See also Appendix, pp. 90-98. *Kelly 1927, 1939;
Charity Commissioners report 1902; WSA 2474/18*

Sutton Veny   At first a reading room was open each winter in a cottage rented
for the season. In 1886 a new cottage was used, the previous one being let for

other purposes. A more substantial building was in use by 1900. In 1911 this was being referred to as the Booker Memorial Hall reading room. *Kelly 1911, 1939; Wiltshire Times 13 Nov 1886; WSA D/398/16*

Swallowcliffe   A recreation room is referred to in 1927 and 1939. *Kelly 1927, 1939*

Teffont Evias   *(pl. 52)* The school (Teffont Manor School) built on the east side of the street opposite Carter's Lane was used as a reading room in 1923 and 1962. It is now a private house. *VCH vol 13; O.S. 6in 1926*

Teffont Magna   *(pl. 53)* A reading room was established in 1886 in a building which had once been a wool store. It seems to have been moved later to a purpose built building containing a single room 36 ft by 18 ft. Permission was given in 1927 for domestic science lessons to be held there for a number of local schools. It is now business premises. *WSA 1254/18; TNA ED70/2579*

Tidworth   A reading room was established at South Tidworth in the 19th century. In about 1900 Sir John Kells sold the reading room (as part of his estate) to the War Office on condition they maintained the exterior. In 1933 North Tidworth Parish Council claimed they also had the right to use the room. Eventually a joint committee was established in 1936. *WSA L7/392/13*

Tisbury   *(pl. 54)* In 1913 a working men's club, reading room and library was built on land beside the school in High Street. The plot of land had been conveyed to the trustees by Lady Arundell for five guineas. A clause in the agreement allowed the pupils from the school to use the building during playtime in bad weather. A substantial library was always a feature of the institute and by 1957 it was being developed as part of the County Library service. *Kelly 1927, 1939; VCH vol 13; WSA 1407/1, 1407/2*

Tollard Royal   In 1890 Pitt-Rivers opened King John's House, formerly a farm house, as an exhibition gallery. A room in the house was also used as a reading room for residents of the parish. By 1907 it had become a private house. *VCH vol 13*

Turleigh   *(pl. 55)* In 1920 Major Leverson Scarth gave the village a club house to be used as a reading room in memory of his wife. The building in Cottles Lane had previously been used as a stable. On the upper floor was a library including Major Scarth's own collection. It was sold in 1973. *Kelly 1939; WCH; 'Turleigh 2000: Portrait of a Wiltshire Village'*

Upavon   *(pl. 56)* In 1911 a reading room was established in commemoration of the coronation of George V. The building was erected on the road to Everleigh on a site given by W. Alexander. Control was in the hands of the vicar, two churchwardens and two members elected at the annual meeting. *Marlborough Times 19 May 1911; Kelly 1927, 1939; WSA 1975/17*

Upton Lovell A reading room is mentioned in 1896. *Wiltshire Times 11 Jan 1896*

Urchfont This reading room was unusual in that it was established in the 1870s by Wadworth Brewery which bought a pair of semi-detached cottages and added a sizeable extension to accommodate a working men's club and reading room. Unlike every other reading room it served alcoholic drinks and was really more of a working men's club. In 1908 (and again in 1910 and 1912) authority was obtained to hold domestic science lessons in the reading room. It was then described as being 50 to 100 yards from the school. It became a private house in the 1920s. *Kelly 1899, 1911; TNA ED70/2537; 'Urchfont: A History of the Parish 2001'*

Warminster Sambourne The Christ Church Reading Room and Working Men's Club was established in 1885 through the efforts of the vicar, Rev. Hickman. It was housed in two converted cottages provided by Lord Bath in Sambourne Road.   The cottages were developed to form one large room 35ft by 14ft which could be partitioned. It was lined with match boarding and new, larger free stone windows were installed. The reading room was still in operation in 1910. *Warminster Journal 3 Oct 1885; Salisbury Journal 3 Oct 1885; Wiltshire Times 1 Oct 1910*

West Ashton In 1884 a reading room and coffee club was opened in a house with four rooms by Lady Doreen and Miss Ethel Long. A village hall and Institute was erected in 1922 by public subscription. *Kelly 1899, 1927; Marlborough Times 4 Oct 1884; Wiltshire Times 31 Oct 1885*

Westwood A reading room is mentioned in 1886. *Wiltshire Times 30 Oct 1886*

Wexcombe A club and reading room was opened in January 1910. This was the gift of Mr. K. McAndrew who also provided firing, lighting, books and games. It was primarily intended for the workers on his estate but it was also open to others in the village. *Marlborough Times 22 Jan 1910*

Whaddon (Alderbury) In 1913 a campaign was launched by Mr. Jervis to raise funds for a building in which mission services and meetings might be held and also serve as a reading and games room. The Earl of Radnor had offered a site and had also promised to meet half of the estimated cost of £300. *WSA 3476/1/2*

Wilton A new reading room, lecture hall and coffee room, supported by the Earl of Pembroke, was opened in 1880. *Wiltshire Times 10 Jul 1880, 12 Feb 1910*

Wingfield A reading and coffee room is mentioned in 1899. *Kelly 1899, 1911, 1927*

Winsley In 1910 a new reading room was opened. It was built by Mr. J. Thornton of Conkwell Grange and rented to the committee. It then had 51 ordinary and 21 honorary members. *Wiltshire Times 12 Nov 1910*

Winterbourne Dauntsey A reading room had been established at some time on the road leading to Winterbourne Gunner. The County Council bought it by compulsory purchase in 1974 for road improvements. *WSA 2035/13*

Winterbourne Stoke In 1935 the reading room in Church Street was converted into a cottage. *WSA G1/760/198; WBR*

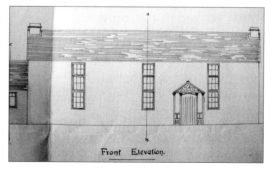

Winterbourne Stoke

Woodborough There is a reference to a reading room in 1883. In 1891 the Rose and Crown Inn was converted to a Temperance Inn and two rooms were knocked together to form a reading room. *Kelly 1880, 1899, 1911, 1927, 1939; Lucy 1883; Wiltshire Times 17 Feb 1883, 31 Oct 1891*

Woodford In December 1884 an entertainment was held in the reading room, organised by the members and their friends. *Salisbury Journal 3 Jan 1885*

Wootton Bassett In 1875 a reading room was opened at Mr. Puce's in the High Street through the effort of Rev. Chase. In 1882 a Workman's Room comprising a reading and quiet recreation room was established in Wood Street. It had about 50 members but it also allowed the Red Star football team to use the premises for its meetings. *Wiltshire Independent 18 Feb 1875; Swindon Advertiser 31 Oct 1885; Wiltshire Times 2 Jan 1886*

Worton *(pl. 58)* The building was erected in 1911 and originally called the Library Hall because it was partly funded by Andrew Carnegie. In 1929 there is a reference to the building having two rooms, the larger of which was used for lettings and the smaller as a reading room. Later this became the village hall. *O.S. 6in 1926; WSA 1516/32; WCH*

Wroughton The first reading room was opened in 1859 as part of the Mutual Improvement Society. It was originally held in the school room in the grounds of Ivery House but a new building was erected in 1865 by the old Ely Inn. This reading room seems to have declined and closed by about 1881. In 1884 a new Reading and Recreation Institute was formed in the old Methodist Chapel (then owned by the church) in the High Street. This was still active in the Second World War but is now a private house. *Swindon Advertiser 14 Nov 1859, 6 Dec 1884, 31 Jan 1885, 19 Dec 1885; North Wilts Herald 23 Jan 1885, 18 Dec 1885; Hilary Dunscombe*

Wylye A coffee room and library was established in 1884 by the Countess of Pembroke and the rector, Rev. Powell. This seems to have been in a cottage provided by the Countess of Pembroke and contained a reading room, a bagatelle room and a refreshment room. By 1890 the reading and recreation room is described as being at the Wyvern Hall. *Wiltshire Times 19 Jan 1884, 26 Jan 1884; Salisbury Journal 22 Feb 1890; WSA 521/37*

Yatesbury There is a reference to a village library in 1883. *Wiltshire Times 22 Sep 1883*

Literature and Sources

Very little has been written about village reading rooms in general. So far the sum total seems to be three articles. In 1990 Owen Stinchcombe published 'Researching Village Reading Rooms' in *The Local Historian* (Vol. 20 no.4 November 1990). This was an offshoot of some work he was doing on the life of Elizabeth Malleson. His study was of Gloucestershire and, in a sense, it was hardly encouraging. He found few primary archival sources and came to the conclusion that it would be necessary to undertake a tedious and extensive trawl through all local newspapers. In the end he managed to build up case histories of only 22 reading rooms with brief notes on about 50 others.

The second article came in 1995 with Nesta Evans 'Reading Rooms in Suffolk' (*Suffolk Review* vol.25 Autumn 1995). The Suffolk Local History Council undertook in 1993 a survey of reading rooms in the county through a questionnaire sent to all their members. This was much more productive with 114 parishes reporting in varying amounts of detail on reading rooms which had existed in their area. This enabled Nesta Evans to undertake a quite detailed analysis of their origins, nature, buildings, activities and their eventual demise.

The most substantial modern research has been done by Carole King. Her unpublished M.A. thesis 'The rise and decline of village reading rooms with particular reference to Norfolk (University of East Anglia 2007)' has been followed with her article 'The Rise and Decline of Village Reading Rooms' (*Rural History* 20, 2009). This covers more of the national background than Evans but otherwise covers the same ground for the county of Norfolk. She has traced some 166 reading rooms and her analysis on their founders, dates of establishment and activities is very similar to that for Suffolk. Perhaps somewhat controversial is her explanations of the reasons for their foundation and of their demise or transformation into village halls. Compared with Stinchcombe, both Evans and King show that reading rooms were numerous and widespread with the peak period of foundation being the 1880s and 1890s. They also refer to a wide range of both primary and secondary material. A study has also been made of reading rooms in the Yorkshire Dales : C. Patrick 'Reading rooms and literary institutes of the Yorkshire Dales' in R.F.White and P.R.Wilson eds. *Archaeology and historic landscapes of the Yorkshire Dales.*

The most important documentary source is the minutes and accounts of the reading room committees. But there is much other archival evidence e.g. maps and plans from planning applications, Charity Commission reports, note books and correspondence. Wiltshire seems to be richer than many other counties with some documentary material on 52 reading rooms. Kelly's Directories are particularly valuable, at least in establishing the existence of some reading rooms, but probably only about a half of the reading rooms which are known to have existed are actually mentioned. The larger scale Ordnance Survey maps also indicate many reading rooms. Then newspapers must be explored. Trying to cover all local papers for the fifty years 1860 to 1910 is a time-consuming and tedious business but immensely rewarding. It is there that one finds detailed reports of the opening of new reading rooms, of the annual meetings and of activities and other events. Individual village histories, many of which were written to celebrate the millennium, may also contain local information on reading rooms not otherwise available.

National background information is sparse and difficult to trace. Stinchcombe refers to two books about reading rooms and experiences of them published by Lady Janetta Manners in 1885 and 1886. These were a reprint of her columns from *The Queen.* King quotes extensively from *A Plea for Reading Rooms in Rural Parishes by a Country Curate* (1862). Evans mentions one piece of evidence produced to the Select Committee on Public Libraries (1849) when Rev. Henry Mackenzie , vicar of St. Martin's in the Fields, advocated the establishment of reading rooms for the working classes to take them away from public houses or their crowded lodgings. Other national evidence is very patchy and arises from almost chance discoveries in newspapers and periodicals. For example, *The Academy,* a London weekly review of literature, science and art, published an article on village reading rooms in 1897 but, rather than extolling them, wrote them down as unattractive and unpopular. A much longer and more supportive article appeared in *Household Words* in 1851. *Punch* had an amusing article in 1861, supposedly from a pub landlord, decrying the new reading rooms and highlighting the better attractions that he could offer. *The Times* in 1855 published a report of a speech by Lord Stanley advocating the establishment of reading rooms 'for facilitating recreation and self-culture among the humbler classes in the rural districts of the country'. This provoked some correspondence notably from a country vicar who said he had tried unsuccessfully to establish a reading room on the Stanley 'town' model and he suggested something less grand and more homely might succeed. There were also caveats about Lord Stanley's scheme being too central and too elaborate for rural areas from C.St. Denys Moxon, curate of Fakenham, and from 'Abnormis Sapiens'. Other random but useful evidence comes from: a long speech by William Gladstone as Chancellor of the Exchequer on the opening of the reading room at Buckley near Mold (*Liverpool Mercury* 5 January 1864); a report on a village reading room near Newcastle (*Newcastle Courant* 11 November 1887); 'Free Reading Rooms' (*The Graphic* 28 February 1885); a meeting to establish a reading room in Montague Street, Bristol (*Bristol Mercury* 27 July 1850).

There was a parallel movement to provide reading rooms for soldiers. The Wiltshire and Swindon Archives is fortunate to have the 1860 correspondence of Florence Nightingale with Sidney Herbert, Secretary for War, firstly trying to persuade him to establish a committee of inquiry into the provision of reading in army barracks and then, when she was successful, her detailed briefing notes on how the committee should proceed.

Altogether one can be much more optimistic than Stinchcombe was in 1990 on there being sufficient material to write about village reading rooms.

Notes

1 Samuel Best *Village Libraries and Reading Rooms* lecture at St.Martin's Hall Education Exhibition Society and Arts 1854.
2 The rules of the Hants and Wilts Educational Society are contained in an appendix to Best.
3 *Bristol Mercury* 27 July 1850.
4 *Lloyds Weekly Newspaper* 14 May 1854
5 *The Times* 26 November 1855
6 *The Times* 1 December 1855
7 *The Times* 30 November 1855
8 *The Times* 6 December 1855
9 *Punch* 12 January 1861
10 *Liverpool Mercury* 5 January 1854
11 *The Times* 4 January 1856
12 The Florence Nightingale correspondence is in the Wiltshire and Swindon Archives WSA 2057/F8/V/C/41
13 *The Times* 30 August 1883

Appendix
Plans and Booklist

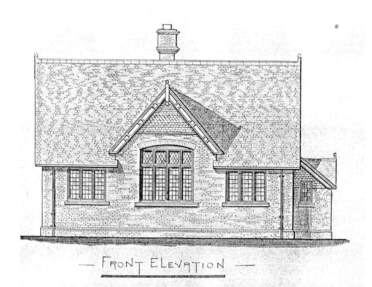

FRONT ELEVATION

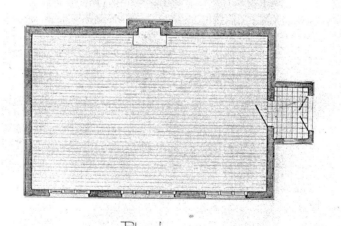

— PLAN —

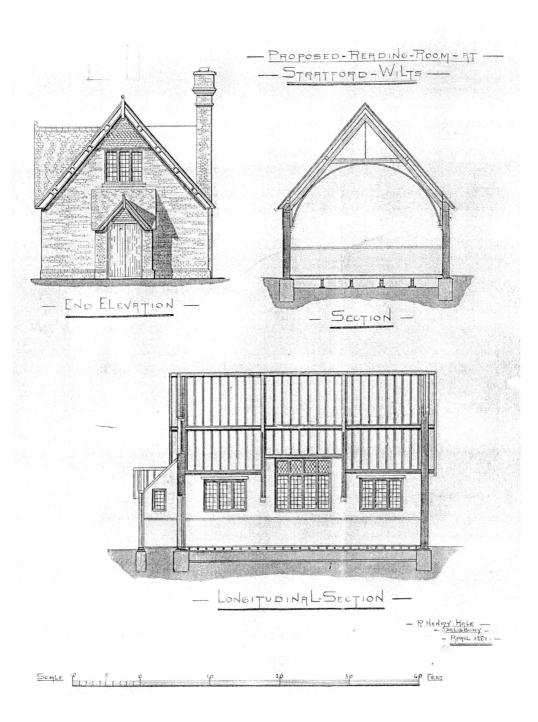

PROPOSED·READING·ROOM·AT
STRATFORD·WILTS

— END ELEVATION —

— SECTION —

— LONGITUDINAL·SECTION —

R. HENRY HALE
SALISBURY
APRIL 1881

SCALE 5 10 20 30 40 FEET

*Above and opposite page: Plans and elevations of Stratford-sub-Castle Reading Room
(courtesy of Gerald Steer)*

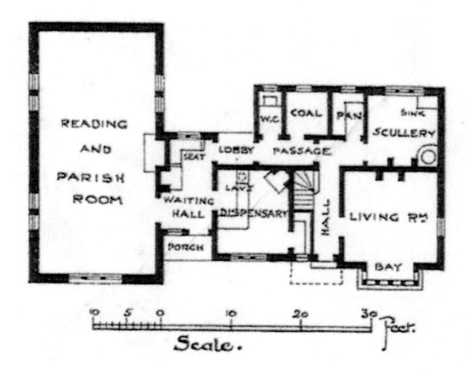

Above: East Kennett Reading Room (enlarged detail from pl. 17)

pages 93-98: list of books, periodicals and games stocked at Stratford-sub-Castle Reading Room, 1886

Copy of Inventory of Books - Furniture, Fixtures
Games &c &c in the Reading Room & Premises on
May 1886 (Books)

Vols		Vols	
1	The Andrews & their Friends	44	Brt &c —
2	Pilgrim Street	1	Mary Sefton
1	Old Blind Ned	1	Shrimp
1	All Golden	1	Short & Sweet
1	Mrs Woodruffes Refuge	1	Jack & Shag
1	Filling up the Chinks	1	Larry Corners Charge
1	City Sparrows	1	Always too late
2	Little Ben Hadden	1	The Ravens Feather
1	A Thorny Path	1	Harry Bwine
1	Golden Mushroom	1	Lost Gip
1	Harolds Choice	1	Little Faith
1	Mark Steadman	1	The Storm of Life
1	Tommie Brown	1	Cassy
1	My Brother Paul	1	No place like Home
1	The Middletons	1	Jessica's first Prayer
1	True to his Bow	1	An Apprentice
1	Especially those by Brenda	1	Hungering & Thirsting
1	Cherry Stones	2	Christie's old Organ
1	Barford Bridge	1	Nobody Cares
1	Hugh Wynford	1	Katies
1	Alone in London	1	Villa of Claudens
1	Michel Lorio Cross	1	Perils of Greatness
1	For Lucy's Sake	1	Harry the Sailor Boy
2	Under the Old Roof	1	Ruth Bloom
1	Patsy	1	Bonward Kendal
1	Worth of a Baby	1	Gilbert Gresham
1	A Night & a Day	1	John's Money Box
1	Old Transom	1	My Scarlet Shawl
1	A Man of his Word	1	Sparrows on the Housetops
11	Very small books for Childn	1	Shaws Farm
1	Soldier Sam	1	Carola

Vols		Vols	
75	No of Vols Brt up	107	No. of Vols Brt up
1	Bede's Charity	2	Paradise Lost
1	Nothing but the Truth	1	Dying Saviour
1	Bramahs Fisheries	1	Sunday Thoughts
1	Parish Magazine	1	Sermon on the Beatitudes
1	Spinster at Home	1	Historical Illustrations of
1	German Home Life		the Old Testament
1	British Reformers	1	Living to purpose
1	In & about London	1	Working for God
1	Alone among the Zulus	1	The last first
1	Guide to the Lakes	1	The Kingdom & the People
1	Twelve years in Canterbury N.Z.	1	Pilgrims Progress
1	Home	1	Sunday Echoes
1	Reading in Engh Literature	1	The Lord is my Shepherd
1	Southern Isles	1	The Night Lamp
1	Worthies of Science		
1	British Islands	1	Sketches by Boz
1	Home Naturalist	1	Coming thro' the Rye
1	Homes Homely & Happy	1	Johnny Ludlow
1	Letters from Sarawak	1	Diary of Kitty Trevylyan
1	Here & there in London	1	Chrons of Schönberg Cotta Family
1	Boy Princes	1	Laneton Parsonage
1	Chapters from French Hist?	1	Faithful & True
1	Peak & Plain	1	Castle Cornet
1	Modern Wonders of World	1	Right & Wrong Way
1	Wonders of the World		
1	Treasury of Hist? & Travel	1	Kings' namesake
1	Till the Doctor comes	1	Brag & Holdfast
1	King Lear	1	Voyage round the World
1	Twelfth Night	1	Without & Within
2	Selections from Poets	1	Margaret's Secret
1	Wiltshire Rhymes	1	Ministry of Life
107	No of Vols carried up	136	No of Vols carried over

Vols		Vols	
136	No of Vols Bt over	173	No of Vols Brot up
1	Leone	1	Gates Ajar
1	By Still Waters	1	Prince of the House of David
1	Last Days of Pompeii	1	Something to do
1	Benlock Chase	1	Triumphs of Perseverance
1	The Brown papers	1	Life Underground
1	Rasselas	1	The Mirage of Life
1	Christie Redforn	1	Life's Pleasure Garden
1	Hall's Vineyard	2	Jessie's Gleanings
1	David Lloyds last Will	1	Romantic Tales
1	My 1st Year in Canada	1	Stones About
3	Mysterious Island	1	Henrietta West
1	Helens Babies	1	Wide Wide World
2	Midshipman Easy	1	Gipsy Breynton
1	Jacob Faithful	1	Faith Gartney
1	Vicar of Wakefield	1	The Revellers
5	Tales from Blackwood	4	Hymn Books
1	Haworths	21	Walter Scotts Novels
1	Erema	8	Andersons Fairy Tales
1	Mine is thine	1	Conscript
1	Young Musgrave	1	Waterloo
1	Bush Life in Queensland	1	Blockade
1	Curate in Charge		
1	Pauline		
1	Heroes & Great Men		
1	Tales about India		
1	Legends & Records		
1	A Hero		
1	Holiday House		
1	Gayworthys		
1	Stepping Heavenward		
173	No of Vols - Carried up	225	No of Vols Carried up

Vols		Vols	
225	No of Vols Brot up	255	No of Vols Brt up
1	English at North Pole	1	Life of Neil D'Arcy
1	London Sparrows	1	Which wins
1	Froggys little brother	1	Uncle Toms Cabin
1	Æsops	1	The Grahams
1	Helens Babies	1	Cage & Singing Birds
1	Kangaroo Hunters	1	British Ferns
1	Hunter the Trapper	1	Grants & How to fight them
1	Foxholme Hall	1	Romantic Incidents
1	Dramatic Readings		in the lives of Naturalists
1	English Hearts & Hands	1	South Sea Whaler
1	British Butterflies	10	Household Words
1	Stories from Jewish Hist.y	3	The Quiver
1	Common Objects of the Country	4	The Childrens Prize
1	Stories of the Gorilla Country	2	Beetons Boys Annual
1	Neds Motto	1	Mistletoe Grange
1	Far off in Asia	1	Profitable Gardening
1	Ungava	1	A Floating City
1	A Chaplt of Stories	1	The Tract Magazine
1	Young Nile Voyageurs	1	On the Banks of the Amazon
1	Johnny & his dog	1	Shipwrecks & Disasters at Sea
1	Wars of England	1	Little Dorrit
1	Little May	1	Gleanings in Natural History
1	Merchants Widow	1	Family Walking Sticks
1	Little Men	5	Sunday at Home
1	Little Women	5	Friendly Greetings
1	Wild man of the West	1	Birthday Gift Book
1	Jack Manly	1	Our Nursery picture Book
1	Lionel's Revenge	1	Paul Parrots picture Book
1	Children of Cloverly	1	Mrs Burtons Best Bedroom
1	Juvenile Missionary Mag	7	Leisure Hour
255	No of Vols carried up	313	No of Vols carried over

Vols		
319	No of vols Brot forward	
2	Books of Fairy Tales	1
1	Golden Hours	
1	Katie Brightside	
1	The Childrens Treasury	
6	Boys own Paper	
10	Day of Rest	
1	Dickens Christmas Books	
1	Graphic	
5	Illustrated London News	
1	Boys own Annual	
13	The Cottager & Artizan	1
19	The British Workman	1
10	Band of Hope Review	1
1	Cassells Art Treasury	
1	Tiger Shooting in India	
386		

Unbound Periodicals & Papers

9 V. + 16 No.	Quiver	
9 Xmas No	Do	
22 No.	Household Words	
16 "	Union Jack	✓
43 .	Girls own paper	
128 "	Wkly Sunday at Home	
4 "	Monthly Do Do	
16 "	Boys own paper	
9 "	Shaws Home Series	1
7 .	Life of Prince Consort	1
11 "	All the year Round	
49 "	Good Words	

A large number of Illustrated & various Periodicals - Papers Tales

5 Scrap Books
1 Map of Dominion of Canada
Cottagers Saturday Night Illustrated

List of Games &c
_____

1 Bagatelle Board with Table, Cues & Balls ✓

1 Musical Cabinet ✓

4 Boxes of Dominoes & 4 Cribbage Boards with Pegs ✓

1 Drawing Slate ✓   1 Slide for Views ✓

1 Peep Show & 12 views ✓   1 Race Game & 1 Fox Hunt in box ✓

3 Chess Boards with 1 set of Chessmen & Draughts 2 sets ✓

Dice & 2 boxes in fox hunt box ✓ Gem Puzzle? 2 Fifteen Puzzles ✓

1 Spelling Game ✓   1 Deer Game ✓

2 Small musical Boxes ✓

5 Glass Ball Puzzle Boards with Balls ✓

1 Thirty Four Puzzle – ✓   1 Spinner

9 Old Bagatelle balls _____ ✓

vols
2 Cassells Hist. of Fr & German War – Vol 1 & 2 presented by Mr T Maundos 87

Index of Civil Parishes

General Index